THE AUTHOR: Lewis Mackenzie (Duncan Lewis Mackenzie Macfarlane) first came to Japan as a child in a ship commanded by his father. After some years as a seafarer, he went ashore and worked in Indonesia and later Australia, where he was employed as a schoolmaster and also wrote verse for the *Sydney Bulletin*. Mackenzie spent several more years at sea before he and his wife moved to Japan in 1936. They lived in Tokyo and Kobe and made numerous excursions into the countryside. After serving in Malaya and New Guinea during World War II, he returned with his wife to Japan and lived in Yokohama from 1947 to 1962, again travelling a great deal in rural Japan. With his friend, Professor Toshio Namba—author of several books in Japanese on Robert Burns—Mackenzie has given talks on the similarities between the poetry of Issa and that of the Scottish poet. He now resides in Britain.

The Autumn Wind

A SELECTION FROM THE POEMS OF ISSA

TRANSLATED AND INTRODUCED BY

LEWIS MACKENZIE

KODANSHA INTERNATIONAL
Tokyo, New York, San Francisco

Previously published by John Murray Ltd., London, in 1957.

Distributed in the United States by Kodansha International/USA Ltd., through Harper & Row, Publishers, Inc., 10 East 53rd Street, New York, New York 10022. Published by Kodansha International Ltd., 12-21, Otowa 2-chome, Bunkyo-ku, Tokyo 112 and Kodansha International/USA Ltd., with offices at 10 East 53rd Street, New York, New York 10022 and The Hearst Building, 5 Third Street, Suite No. 430, San Francisco, California 94103. Copyright © 1984 by Kodansha International Ltd. All rights reserved. Printed in Japan.
LCC 83-48874
ISBN 0-87011-657-6
ISBN 4-7700-1157-1 (in Japan)
First paperback edition, 1984

ACKNOWLEDGMENTS

Although he has not seen my manuscript, Doctor Sanki Ichikawa was kind enough to make some valuable suggestions regarding it, particularly relating to the translation of the names of flowers and insects. I am very grateful to him. Professor Yasuo Yamato of Nihon University has performed the truly onerous task of reading my translations and, while there could be no kindlier critic, he found many misreadings to correct. He also explained many obscurities and suggested English equivalents with the sense of poetry and of word values that one would expect from the translator of *Endymion*. My hearty thanks are due to him and to his assistant, Professor Toshio Namba. Mr Yuzo Yamamoto has also helped me with the interpretation of some of Issa's colloquial phrases.

It was a reading of Professor H. G. Henderson's book *The Bamboo Broom* which first drew my attention to Issa and led me eventually to read some of the original texts. The book, of which I understand a revision has been prepared, remains for me a marvel of brevity and charm, like many of the *haiku* it embodies, and the author's rhymed translations have most memorable qualities, so far inadequately noticed. Professor Henderson has been kind enough to read my manuscript and he has made some welcome and constructive criticisms. I would express my thanks also to Mr R. H. Blyth and his two works—the compendious *Haiku* in four volumes with a wealth of commentary, and the brilliant *Senryu*, at once so witty and so illuminating. Nobody who attempts to transfer the thoughts expressed by the *haiku* poets into a European language should be without the former. I have quoted from it in the Introduction.

The headman of Kashiwabara village, Mr Wakatsuki, gave me much courteous assistance during a visit which I made to the Issa country last year, and I have found his compilation, *Issa Matsuri*, most useful, containing as it does a number of essays on different aspects of the poet's life and work.

My thanks are also due to Lady Bouchier and to Mr Stephen Shaw of Kodansha International for making this edition possible and to the late Mr Ceadel and Mr Kamibayashi for pointing out in their reviews errors and possible inaccuracies in the text, most of which have been corrected. I must also thank my old friend, Mr R. Kafuku, for several useful suggestions. I would also like to thank the staff of Kodansha International for pointing out some misreadings.

The spelling 'Edo' has been used throughout for the name of the city which is now known as Tokyo, but 'Yedo' may be more familiar to some readers.

CONTENTS

INTRODUCTION

This book is about a Japanese known as Issa, sometimes with the addition of his surname of Kobayashi. He wrote poetry, mainly in the short verse form called *haiku*, during fifty years of his life which spanned almost equally the eighteenth and nineteenth centuries. I would not claim that my book is in any way comprehensive, but I have sought to present by selection a sample of Issa's *haiku*. Nor, where so much is uncertain, would I claim absolute accuracy, but within these limits I shall try to show some of the reasons that make Issa both respected and beloved by so many of his countrymen, and to pass on something of the message of compassion and fortitude, innocence and faith, he had for the world. As to the honour given to him in his own country, it should be of interest in the West to know that blunt honest speech, impatience with orthodoxy, a universal sympathy and hatred of all forms of pretension, are some of the qualities for which Issa is remembered and admired in Japan. As to the content of his poetry, I have deliberately used the unfashionable word 'message' because poetry was certainly for him a means of communication, and, despite all the complex functions since ascribed to it, for us it must be the same.

An admirable account of the origins and historical development of *haiku* has appeared in Dr Keene's *Japanese Literature*. To it, I would wish to add nothing. It is sufficient to say here that the *haiku*, with its five-seven-five syllable lines, grew out of the opening stanza of the *renga*, or series of linked verses. This explains its fragmentary nature and the sense it gives of leading one on to draw conclusions or to supply what is unexpressed, somewhat in the manner in which the eye and the mind follow a silhouette or stencilled drawing. It also explains the impact of fresh thoughts and images which the best *haiku* can make on the receptive mind. Within itself the *haiku* strives to capture, by antithesis or otherwise, a 'moment of truth' or of revelation. This Dr Keene aptly likens to the leap of an electric spark from pole to pole. It can achieve economically and frequently with great force what is done in the West only by elaborate simile or metaphor.

Thus Issa expresses his indifference to the might and opulence of the wealthiest of Japan's noblemen, Maeda, Lord of Kaga.

> What's that to me,
> His million bales at harvest?
> Dew on a grass stalk! (1)

And again, he tells thus of the puissance of time and fate.

> The autumn wind!
> The mountain's shadow
> Trembles before it. (2)

The revelation is usually announced by *ya* or *zo* or some other 'cutting word' which in reading requires a slight pause.

The *haiku* is, of course, related in form to the *tanka*, which exceeds it in length by a couplet of seven-syllable lines and in which the potential, to maintain the electric figure, is usually between the initial three lines which may themselves be taken as a *haiku*, and this final couplet. It is appropriate also to mention the *senryu*, identical in form with the *haiku*, but dependent for its effect on wit of a shrewd and often cynical quality.

(1) Nan no sono, hyakumangoku mo sasa no tsuyu
(2) Akikaze ya hyoro hyoro yama no kageboshi

Because the *senryu's* sharp tilts at pomposity and man's pretences were so closely akin to a part of himself, Issa's more humorous or rueful comments on life are hard to distinguish from *senryu*. There is usually, however, some touch of the tenderness or grace that he made peculiarly his own to lead the mind on from his pleasantry after the smile has gone.

> As years go on,
> The Dog hardly sniffs it—
> The first lined garment. (3)

Since Chamberlain called it 'the Japanese epigram', the attitude of the West towards *haiku* in general has varied between adulation and belittlement. The facility with which syllables are strung together and the vast number who attempt the stringing have created the impression that where there is so much versifying there can be little or no poetry. There seems to be as little point in blaming *haiku* because they lack the rich diversity of form that dresses the poetry of some other languages, as in blaming a sonnet sequence for being what it is. The limits that have been set to the matter are sometimes to be regretted; but it is a part of the manner, and there is no reason why we should not respect the poets for their acceptance of these limits and turning them to their own high purpose. In *haiku* even English versions show much variety of mood and emphasis.

From among those that most readily turn into English I have chosen some that are likely to convey Issa's quality to a Western reader. It must be admitted that his kindest critics have said that in Issa's verse there is much that is mediocre and monotonous. Moreover, perhaps no other verse-form

(3) Toshi yoreba inu mo kaganu zo hatsu awase

3

when turned into English tends to lose itself so readily in flatness or to lean so far towards self-parody. It is, then, with some diffidence that the translations in this book are put forward, and if they do not communicate anything of significance, they, and not the originals, must be at fault. In reading them, it is necessary of course to remember that direct statements are seldom made of the major concept, but only of its reflection, as it were, in the 'world of appearances'. This is less true of Issa indeed than of others, but it does explain why we can often see no more in *haiku* than dainty pictures.

> Softly the dew descends,
> Softly as pitying tears—
> Doves murmur orisons.   (4)

There indeed is the picture; there is left in the mind the tranquillity of a temple court in the stillness of early morning when together with the least sounds the soft murmuring of the doves is an invocation, and the listener answers in his heart with humble reverence. But, as my friend Professor Henderson has reminded me, '*horori-horori to*' is not merely onomatopoeic. It implies a 'being moved to compassion', so that the lines suggest the impulse towards the divine that springs from 'the pitying heart that felt for human woe'.

In Mr Enright's entertaining book *The World of Dew* he seemed to say that the *haiku* can be no more than a vignette, often charming, but of pictorial interest and nothing more. He has doubtless suffered from the attitude of hushed reverence that they can evoke, and his cheerful irreverence is indeed a natural response; perhaps the chapter entitled 'And yet, and yet . . .' is in some sense an apology. But against his general

(4) Tsuyu horori horori to hato no nebutsu kana

4

estimate of *haiku* I would set the one of Issa's from which he takes his title. It was written after the death of little Sato-jo, the poet's idolised daughter and the third of his children to die in infancy. Issa was then well known and living in his own country, and friends doubtless offered the usual formalities of consolation with pious allusion to the transience of human existence. If they did not, these would certainly have occurred to Issa himself.

> The world of dew—
> A world of dew it is indeed,
> And yet, and yet . . .   (5)

That and no more he wrote, and how much of poignancy it conveys! Or Basho's verse on the field where the gallant young Yoshitsune, victor of so many passages of arms, met defeat and death.

> Grasses of summer—
> From dreams of proud warriors
> These only remain.   (6)

The master of the *haiku* is generally considered to be Basho (1644–1694), who rescued it from conceit and witticism and infused into verses of this mode that spirit of real poetry which often informs them still. With him, poetry was in truth a consecration and a way of life. In his *haiku* we may observe the ceaseless interplay of the temporal and the eternal, the depiction of which Basho proclaimed as one of the prime functions of poetry. He was a great and inspiring teacher and had a multitude of followers, among them major poets in their own

(5) Tsuyu no yo wa tsuyu no yo nagara sari nagara
(6) Natsugusa ya tsuwamonodomo no yume no ato

right, yet after his death the writing of *haiku* degenerated rapidly, on the one hand into a matter of verbal dexterity, on the other into blind conformity with precedent. Buson (1715–1783) was the next great figure who rescued the *haiku* from sterility. No doubt because he was a painter of some note he took an obvious delight in the images his lines reflect and he paid much attention to technique. His images are clear and beautiful, yet nearly all have an air of eternal freshness to awaken or enliven the imagination.

> The temple bell—
> Perched on it, slumbering,
> A butterfly! (7)

Buson died at Kyoto in 1783 when Issa was a young man at Edo and there is no record that they met. Buson's influence was felt most in the old Imperial capital, which had gained in culture as it lost in political power, and among leisured people. There seems to be little evidence that it affected the turbulent community of letters at Edo which was producing a lively torrent of wit, lampoon and erotica. The schools which clung to Basho's principles did so with timidity and little perception. They attached importance to abstruse unities rather than to that contact with life on which Basho had declared one end of poetry's bridge must rest. Issa, although in his own day he occupied a position hardly comparable to that of either Basho or Buson, was by his influence to restore *haiku* poetry to many of its high offices of heart and mind and to charge it with new force. He was to bring it out of the temple and study into fields, kitchens and counting-houses. Remembrances of a highland youth, preserved through weary years of city life,

(7) Tsurigane ni tomarite nemuru kocho kana

6

were to impart to much of his thought a wide untrammelled movement like the flight of a bird over mountain precipices, and were to confirm him in his disregard for the distinctions of society. By expressing sympathy with many sentient creatures other than man he was to say much of man himself while gently pleading the cause of less fortunate neighbours. Looking at the peasant with respect and understanding, he would celebrate the essential decency of hard manual toil. He was to be known as an eccentric, yet no poet sang of matters nearer to the centre of man's being. Finally and pre-eminently, throughout a life filled with affliction, he was to remind men of the mighty movements of time and fate, and by light half-humorous asides to commend to them courage and resignation. To the end he had a cheerful and endearing interest in the smallest matters of daily life. Thus, two verses written before his death in the small storehouse he occupied when his house was destroyed make use of the same object to very different ends.

> 'Who's that?' I say,
> Even when our Dog comes—
> Out of my quilts.   (8)

> A blessing indeed—
> This snow on the bed-quilt,
> This, too, is from the Pure Land.   (9)

*   *   *

(8) Inu ga kite mo donata zo to mosu fusuma kana (Some texts omit the word *mo* which makes it a little uncertain whether the question was Issa's or the dog's. But I think the intention was to express the tedium of long illness and the importance taken on by the smallest incident.)

(9) Arigata ya fusuma no yuki mo Jodo yori

The child to be known as Issa was born at Kashiwabara, a village of the mountainous country of northern Shinano (now Nagano) in the year 1763, thus four years after 'a lad was born in Kyle' whom at some points he would strongly resemble. His father, a yeoman farmer named Yagobei Kobayashi, had fairly extensive lands, cleared and uncleared, and added to his income by carting and hiring out pack-horses. He was a man of some education and literary taste; feckless, complacent, and weak, as we may judge from his conduct of the household, he was yet able to inspire deep affection in those around him. His wife, named Kuni, was the daughter of a headman and substantial farmer at the neighbouring hamlet of Ninokura. She was, it would seem, gentle and under-standing, but capable, as a farm housewife had to be, about the business of the household. With them lived the father's mother, Kanajo. From his birth she doted on this first grand-child, who was given the 'young name' of Yataro.

He was born on 5th May, the day of the Iris Festival when carp banners are still flown over every Japanese household blessed with sons. However, although his birth was a source of great gratification to his parents, no banner flew from their homestead to mark the occasion.

In that country, snow and frost obstruct the farmers' work for so much of the year that the sowing and reaping of the rice has to be crowded into the period between April and October. Hence, early May is the busiest time of all, when one might ask 'even a cat to lend a paw' with the back-breaking task of setting out shoots, and Issa tells us that around his cradle, instead of lullabies, there sounded the planting song.

The country around Kashiwabara and neighbouring Lake Nojiri has a character of its own which we must consider,

8

since although he was absent from the district for most of his life it was seldom altogether absent from Issa's mind. At Nagasaki, far away in the mild south country, he was to write as his New Year verse in 1794.

> First of the year—
> The dream showed me my old Village
> Through a veil of tears! (10)

Few indeed can have apostrophised their birthplace more often than Issa with his innumerable verses beginning 'My old village' (*Furusato ya*)—many of which, however, are bitter comments on the dour nature of those who lived in it. Furthermore, it is certain that the stern brooding grandeur of the natural scene that first met his eyes, the wide upland skies, and the rich variety of the seasons that he watched in those early years, made a lasting impression on him.

It is, then, a country of great beauty. The little broken plain which includes the villages of Kashiwabara and Nojiri is bounded to west and north by the three rounded massive summits of Myoko, Kurohime and Iizuna, while between these last two can be seen the craggy peak of Togakushi. To the east, the deep water of Lake Nojiri is set about with wooded hills. Mountains dominate the villages but do not overshadow them, and the wayfarer is surprised by glimpses of the blue lake from the low hills on each side of the Kashiwabara road. Well-grown trees and, in spring and summer, flowers there are in almost endless variety; graceful birches with silvery bark, dark feathery conifers, tall beeches so bright in springtime, and even the proud and lovely star magnolia. Birds, in the 'open months', are numerous and full of song.

(10) Hatsuyume ni furusato wo mite namida kana

But, for half the year, the land lies silent under snow, and it is not only human activity that has to be crowded into the remainder. Plants, too, adapt themselves to this sudden growth, as Issa tells us.

> The nine-belled flower
> Here bears only four or five bell-blossoms
> And that's all! (*11*)

Because it was on an important route from the north, the village of Kashiwabara had then unexpected political importance. It was just a day's journey each way to the next practicable stage, some distance to the north was the guarded barrier of the province of Echigo, while to the southward was a pass and a forest through which travellers rarely ventured during hours of darkness. These circumstances led to the establishment of a staging post, an inn where great noblemen with their trains could be lodged, and Kashiwabara in consequence was visited by travellers of all kinds from professional wrestlers to dramatists, from amateur essayists to sworded gentlemen adventurers, to a degree surprising for a mountain village. Furthermore, on account of its vital importance as a centre of routes between great feudatories, the autocratic and usually able Tokugawa government made the little village a part of the Shogun's own territories, directly under the administration of Edo. These things all influenced Issa's career and in varying degree they are reflected in his work. But, in a special sense, it is his personal life which caused him to write as he did; some are indeed of the opinion that, without its vicissitudes, little of his poetry would have merited survival.

All seemed to be set fair for the boy Yataro as the eldest son

(*11*) Kurinso shigorinso de shimai-keri

of a prosperous yeoman. But a long tale of misfortune for him began with his young mother's death when he was only three years old. Memories of her sympathy and understanding deepened for him with the years as he found the world less kind, and they probably passed beyond anything actually remembered into an idealised vision. Although his grandmother looked after the child fondly, it seems that to the years immediately following his mother's death Issa traced in himself that awareness of the essential solitude of men and women and of the limitation of human relationships which pervades many of his verses.

> Heedless of the dew
> That marks our closing day
> We bind ourselves to others. (12)

Years afterwards, looking out over the changing and changeless pattern of the waves, he was to write:

> O Mother, whom I lost!
> Every time I watch the sea
> Yes—every time . . . (13)

Despite her love for him and her care, without which, Issa tells us, he would not have survived, his grandmother was doubtless withdrawn and occupied by thoughts of her own.

> O winds of autumn!
> Nearer we draw to the Buddha
> As the years advance. (14)

(12) Mi no ue no tsuyu to mo shirade hodashikeri
(13) Naki-haha ya umi miru tabi ni miru tabi ni
(14) Akikaze ya hotoke ni chikaki toshi no hodo

His father mourned deeply and, it would seem sincerely, for O Kuni yet found little to say to Yataro and before long was to seek another wife.

By his own account Issa then became a peculiar child, outwardly sullen, inwardly nursing a sensibility and thoughts beyond his years. He found it difficult to play with the village children, who, in turn, mocked him for his oddness and even, he says, for being an orphan. It was in recollection of this period that he wrote one of the two verses by which he is known most widely.

> Come then, come hither;
> Play your games and bide with me,
> Motherless sparrow. (15)

The other, as celebrated and now, unfortunately, as hackneyed, is of a later period, when Issa looked down on an uneven duel in Musashi, that home of swordsmen—

> Lean frog,
> Don't you surrender!
> Here's Issa by you. (16)

It throws much light on his temperament to note that Issa speaks of his loneliness in those years before the hostility of a stepmother began to thrust him out from the family circle. It is also of interest, if there is anything more than fancy in the invitation to the sparrow, that despite his own rather morbid self-portrait he suggests that sorrow led him thus early to sympathy with others as luckless. He tells us that he spent whole days alone in the woods and fields at this time, and as

(15) Ware to kite asobeya oya no nai suzume
(16) Yase-gaeru makeru na Issa kore ni ari

12

he sometimes seems to blame himself later for a lack of good fellowship', so his distance from others of his own age caused him disquiet. Consolation was at hand, first in his school studies which he took to with great zest, and then in poetry.

When he was six years old, Yataro went to a school in Kashiwabara kept by Rokuzaemon Nakamura, the master of the staging inn. This Nakamura was known as a calligrapher and mathematician. He lectured to his pupils on the Buddhist scriptures, wrote verses under the name Shimpo, and had a flourishing wholesale business in wine. A passage from an essay of his which has survived in praise of the countryside round Kashiwabara is in an easy dignified style and shows evidence of close observation of the year's changes. This unusual village schoolmaster had another writer of verse, well versed in Chinese composition, to assist him in the school so that it is not altogether strange that Yataro, already prone to musing and solitude, should have found his short school years inspiring. From the first, Nakamura recognised his gifts and remained the poet's life-long friend, encouraging and supporting him in days of adversity, and he was succeeded in this by his two sons. Issa soon gave proof of diligence and, so tradition runs, gained a reputation in the village even at this early age for scholarship and ready wit. A story of that time discredited by the authorities, none the less shows us (like Bruce's spider and Alfred's cakes) the kind of thing by which he came to be remembered.

He is said to have been accompanying a mounted *samurai* of Kaga's household over the lower slopes of Kurohime (Dark Maiden), leading one of his father's pack-horses. As the peak came into sight it was seen that the first thin snows of winter had settled on it. The gentleman was heard to murmur

'*Kurohime ya—Kurohime ya . . .*', evidently feeling that the occasion demanded something poetical. Whereupon Yataro is said to have declaimed.

> The Dark Maiden too—
> Are her thoughts perhaps of love
> In that flossy bridal snood?   (17)

As Mr Bickerton says, a precocious performance indeed! It may here be remarked that several of the verses by which Issa is most widely known in Japan are not accepted as his by scholars. On the other hand, some which are absent from his written works seem to have been preserved by those who knew him well and I have quoted them here in their places. They include his famous farewell or 'death verse' which it was the duty of every poet of old Japan to have ready. The record asserts that death when it came left Issa no time to recite his.

When Issa was eight years old, his father married again and the coming of the stepmother, Satsu, marked a further stage in his misfortunes. She has been execrated by tradition for not showing him more kindness, but being what they were it would have been strange had there been much sympathy between the two. Satsu was a tough-fibred 'managing' woman of hard-working peasant stock who meant to make a success of the farm, while not sparing toil or hardship for herself or others. Her single-minded devotion to toil would have made her a model of excellence in the eyes of the Shogunate which frequently had occasion to reprove the farmers about this time for tastes and pursuits above their station. It would have been surprising if she had not soon lost patience with the silent Yataro, mooning about the yards, practising characters even

(17) Kurohime mo iroke zuita ka wataboshi

14

in the hearth ashes, and chanting verse or Chinese apophthegms as he shook out the fodder. At first she did little more than scold the grandmother for spoiling him and cut down some of his small indulgences. Then not unnaturally she came to resent the time he spent on studies and eventually prevailed on his father to take the boy away from the school. The friendly Nakamura protested more than once, but in vain. Yataro continued to go to him by stealth for teaching on holidays and as often as he could during the 'closed months', but he was kept labouring about the farmstead all day, and at night had to make straw sandals, while as a further refinement of cruelty Satsu would not allow him light by which to read or write. The vexation of this to a boy anxious to study during the long winter evenings of Shinano, together with the day's over-exacting labour, remained to sear his memory all his life.

> O world of men!
> Even for writing on a leaf—
> Again a scolding! (18)

His stepmother's dislike he returned in kind—

> Somebody you do resemble—
> The face, at least, is much the same
> Death adder! (19)

It is remarkable that despite all these difficulties he should have persevered with his studies to have become an acknow-ledged master of composition both in verse and prose.

The school itself was held at the staging-inn (*honjin*) and it therefore afforded him many glimpses of the world outside

(18) Hito no yo ya ko no ha kaku sae shikaruru
(19) Dare yara ga omo ni mo nitaru mamushi kana

the glen. One of the most dramatic was when the magnificent train of Maeda, Lord of Kaga, passed the gates of Nakamura's establishment, on one of that nobleman's progresses between his seat at Kanazawa and the Shogun's capital at Edo. The procession, as that of the most wealthy of all the *daimyo* whose title passed into a byword for ostentation, was in a fixed and well-known order which we may see in the prints of Hiro-shige and, from the great lantern banners to the baggage guard in the rear, it stretched for some six hundred yards. Stern files of pacing men-at-arms guarded the litter which was preceded by sharp-voiced heralds commanding obedience and respect. At their cry 'Down with you!' the populace were expected to bow and sit at the roadside in respectful attitudes until the procession passed. Legend relates that Yataro, awed by this threatening splendour, watched from a safe distance and afterwards recorded his impressions thus:

> Following in his train
> Come the mists that swirl and trail—
> Kaga-no-Kami! (20)

> The plum flower crest
> Here it comes on the great lanthorns
> —Rising from the mist (21)

The plum flower is the device of the Maeda family. He was to write again with less reverence of the same grandee.

At home, the birth of her own son, Senroku, in 1772 changed his stepmother's severity into active malevolence, probably because she resented the place which Issa occupied

(20) Ato tomo wa kasumi hikikeri Kaga-no-Kami
(21) Ume bachi no daichochin ya kasumi kara

16

as heir. In addition to his other tasks he now had to attend constantly on the infant, who seems to have been puling and sickly, and was blamed whenever it cried, which was very often. More than once the woman tried to alienate him from his father by flinging wild accusations at him, but, in spite of Yagobei's infatuation, she failed. Every filial gesture Yataro made toward his father was however fiercely resented. When he was fourteen his grandmother died and the last restraint was removed.

He wrote afterwards that he was beaten every day and 'never slept without shedding tears'. His refuge once again was in the open air and in the society of the great trees about the village. At the Suwa Shrine he came to look on the great pines and chestnut trees which had stood about the precincts for centuries as silent but benevolent presences, and he tells us that he passed a whole night in weeping beneath the steps of the Myosenji Temple.

Even Yagobei at last came to realise something of what the boy was suffering and decided that it would be better if Yataro were sent away from home. His wife might forget her hatred if its object were absent for a time. Accordingly, very early one morning in the spring of 1776, Yataro and his father left the house secretly and joined a company of travellers on their way to the capital. Yagobei accompanied the party as far as the neighbouring town of Mure. There they sat down on the roadside grass and took leave of each other. 'Eat nothing harmful,' said the father, 'don't let people think any ill of you, and let me soon see your bonny face again.' One wonders more at the inadequacy of this valediction than at Yataro's response, for in writing about it afterwards he says that he sat in silence for some time, nodded vigorously, and then bowed his farewell. At fourteen, his kind does not ask for explanations.

As the caravan, with its echoing horse-bells and Yataro bravely trudging along beside it, disappeared over the hill from Yagobei's eyes and wound on towards the temple city of Zenkoji, so Issa disappears from ken for the next ten years. He reached Edo and was no doubt bewildered by the din and fume of that turbulent city and the strange sharp speech of its volatile cockneys, the Edokko. His father had given him a letter of introduction to a relative of his mother's, a literary man who lodged students at his establishment in return for hack-work and copying, but for some unknown reason Issa did not enter this eminently suitable household. Instead, he writes that he often knew what it was to be hungry and cold during those early days in Edo and was hard put to it to find a shelter.

> Floating weeds,
> As blow the winds of the floating world—
> Drifting and drifting.   (22)

On very scanty evidence it has been suggested that he worked as stable boy at one of the great mansions of the *daimyo*, or that he was attached as a paid acolyte doing clerical work at a Buddhist temple.

> They sleep
> In new mosquito nets—
> Horses at Edo   (23)

is headed 'A mansion at Edo'. His writings, moreover, have a

(22) Ukigusa ya ukiyo no kaze no iu mama ni
(23) Atarashiki kaya ni nerunari Edo no uma

18

great many references to the priesthood—sometimes mischievous but not always unkindly—such as the following.

> The temple so clever
> At raking in the money—
> It has the peonies!   (24)

Issa is later found to have numerous friends in priestly orders and afterwards he wrote of a visit to a temple in Shikoku where he expected to find one of them, Sarai, with whom he had shared some of the hardships of the early days in Edo.

There was more to astonish a country boy about the capital of the Shogun than the luxury in which high-bred horses slept. It is evident that the clamour of the turbulent city, with all its ostentation, corruption and complacency, had profound effects on his life and work. Edo had changed greatly from the fortress city which the first great Tokugawa, Iyeyasu, set up. A huge community of merchants, craftsmen and entertainers had assembled to serve the needs of the *daimyo*, all of whom maintained mansions there; there were the multitudinous officials of the administration virtually doubled by the system of censors or 'attached eyes'; and the army of *hatamoto*, or direct retainers of the Shogun, who had resided permanently at Edo during these long years of peace and whose maintenance was frequently an embarrassment to the Government. Furthermore, the peculiar custom of '*yabu-iri*' (literally, and to use an Australianism, 'going bush') added every year to the number of townsmen. By this system, in theory, servants were changed and apprentices finished their time every spring, when, like Issa's, new parties of young men and women arrived from the country seeking employment. Those they

(24) Kane moke jozu na tera no botan kana

replaced were expected by the Government to return to their farms, but frequently, again like Issa, they did not return after their two or three years of city life; many became mere hangers-on as *yamabushi* ('wandering priests') or *bikuni* ('priestesses'), euphemisms which, as a striking sign of the times, were widely used to cover less respectable employment. But the largest element in the city was also the least productive. Together with their households, gentlefolk who wore two swords and were debarred from the useful pursuits of trade so long as they wore them and claimed their rice, sometimes numbered, according to one historian, as much as one-third of Edo's population. Iyeyasu had laid down a proud code for their behaviour and this, like his political system, was still there to be admired. The system, like a well-oiled machine, could and did survive incompetence in the ruling classes; but the code relied on repressions and austerities repugnant to many worthy people without the inspiration of war, philosophy or religion. The reaction had been a violent one, so that idle *samurai* frequently became bankrupt and fell into disreputable courses to maintain themselves in luxury and ostentation. 'Knightly faith' had become for many a mockery; and the order on whom it has been enjoined were now more often seen in theatres and licensed quarters than exercising their arms. Some provinces had maintained good government and ordered society, but circumstances made the position far otherwise at Edo.

When Issa arrived to stare at the wonders of the capital, matters were in a particularly bad way. The great Shogun, Yoshimune, had been successful in arresting much of the deterioration in society and particularly in steadying the people's livelihood, even at Edo; his work, however, was largely undone by the incompetence or indifference of his successors, Iyeshige and Iyeharu. Under both, corrupt ministers debased almost every function of Government itself and not until the regency of Sadanobu, some ten years later, when a series of appalling natural disasters strained the country to breaking-point, was any real effort to be made at reform. Well might Issa write:

> Don't mention people—
> Even the very scarecrows,
> Crooked, every one! (25)

He also had many comments on *yabu-iri* and its unsettling effects:

> The Servants Day—
> The house-dog also sees them off
> Into the mists. (26)

> He can't hide them
> His white hairs now—
> At Yabu-iri. (27)

Issa wrote that *samurai* and townsmen scrabbled for a living, like birds fighting over corn, using by turns bluster and guile to better themselves at the expense of fellow-creatures.

The exuberance of the Genroku age at the end of the seventeenth century had brought about a rich flowering of art,

(25) Hito wa iza sugu na kakashi mo nakari keri
(26) Yabu-iri ya inu mo mi-okuru kasumu made
(27) Yabu-iri no kakushi kanetaru shiraga kana

literature and the theatre. By Issa's time this had largely passed, with society in a bitter disillusioned mood, into extravagance and decay. However, it must be remembered that just as there were many great families who even at this time maintained and fostered the finer traits of the *samurai*, and stalwart townsmen who stood manfully against oppression and debauchery, much qualification of any such general statement is necessary. Even in Tokugawa Japan, human activity never really conformed to one pattern. While a spate of books was produced which are remarkable only for banality and pornography, weighty commentaries and concordances were also written on the ethical philosophies of China and the ancient Japanese texts. For scholars, indeed, it was an age of commentary. Similarly in poetry, along with an inordinate flood of poetising which kept professional 'markers' busy, there were a few schools which occupied themselves in analysing the minutiae of Basho's table talk and in fiercely condemning compositions that did not conform to the rules which, sometimes on doubtful evidence, the Master was thought to have laid down.

I have dwelt on conditions at Edo because the contrast with the simple village life he had known must have affected Issa's life and thought no less than his early departure from home and the long bitter quarrel with his relatives which ensued. For thirty-seven years the city was to be his base and, although during that time he travelled much about Japan, this is a much longer period than he ever spent in Shinano. In spite of himself, it is plain that he came to like something of Edo's thoughtless vitality, its cheerful bustle and even the impudent conceit it had of itself.

No house he had
But he passed the New Year
At Edo! (*28*)

But he never ceased to proclaim himself a countryman, and by his frugal example to exclaim against the luxury and artificiality of the town. It has been rather unkindly suggested that he took the part of rustic poet because imitation cits of literary bent were already so numerous. However, rather than being a deliberate pose, it is likely that his outlook and actions arose naturally out of diversity of temperament. The typical Edokko, as we can still see him vigorously and colourfully presented on the Kabuki stage, was noisy and gay, quarrelsome and improvident, rushing to extravagance in word and deed, and infected by a rather comic disdain for all things outside his city. To these must be added virtues of resilience, courage, and good humour.

Thanks to the blossoms!
On ground that they've shaded
No one's a stranger! (*29*)

—was written by Issa himself about Edo when brightly clad crowds of townsfolk met 'on a Sunshine Holyday' to toast the cherry blossoms of Ueno, with wine and merriment. This he found pleasing enough, but the stridency of Edo life repelled him.

(*28*) Iye nashi mo Edo no ganjitsu shitarikeri
(*29*) Hana no kage aka no tanin wa nakari keri (I had translated this as 'Under the blossoms | there were no strangers' but Professor Henderson reminded me of the two common meanings of *kage*—namely 'shadow' and '[by] favour [of]'. Whether both are intended or not they certainly add to the force of the poem.)

To a country boy, already moody and diffident, moving for the first time outside his family circle, this was not unnatural. Even the language, like Cockney to a Yorkshire man, would baffle him with its clipped slang and sharp twisted vowels. He was teased for his slow highland speech and perhaps this did more to influence him than has been thought.

> Country starling, country starling!
> People gird and sneer and jabber—
> How cold it is tonight!   (30)

> In all Edo,
> You've the first and finest voice, of course,
> O cuckoo!   (31)

Never had a youth more reason to dislike the farmer's life, and even when he had his own land there is no record that he worked it. Like that of many another exile, separation quickened his loyalty and nobody can have written with more familiar sympathy of farm and field.

> Youngster pulling turnips
> Claps on and heaves with might and main—
> Then topples over!   (32)

> The peasant girl—
> Pickaback on her shoulder
> Sleeps a butterfly!   (32A)

Whatever his first employment was in Edo he managed to

(30) Mukudori to iu hito sawagu yosamu kana
(31) Edoiri no ichiban koe zo hototogisu
(32) Daiko hiki hyoshi ni korori kozo kana (The *daiko*[n] is not of course a turnip but a giant radish.
(32A) Saotome ni obusatte nemuru kocho kana

24

continue his studies and, during scanty leisure, even to associate with those who were writing verses. There is a tradition that he was nineteen when he entered the Katsushika school, one of those bound by strict rule and convention, which had been founded by a close friend of Basho but which had not at the time a high reputation. His earliest conjectural verse dates from this year, having been found in the visitors' book of a country hermitage.

> Doffing my broad hat—
> How they shrilled through my ears,
> Voices of insects! (*33*)

With the year 1787, we move into certainty, for his signature is then found appended to a handwritten book—written as Kobayashi Ikyo—which was copied by students of the Katsushika school as a part of their studies. A remarkable tribute to his talent then appears—or perhaps it was to the thoroughness with which he had mastered the conventions he was so soon to surpass. His teacher, Nirokuan Chikua, died, and Issa as a young man of twenty-eight was elected to succeed him. He did so, and taught with the name Nirokuan Kikumei. But, if this early success attests to his gifts, the fact that it could not content him and was soon abandoned speaks even more eloquently of his integrity. Critics cite verses such as the following from his brush to show how he had drilled his genius under the Katsushika rule.

> There, under the cloud,
> The white cloud of the cherry flowers
> There is Toyama! (*34*)

(*33*) Kasa torite mimi ni shimiiru ya mushi no koe
(*34*) Shiragumo no sakura wo kuguru Toyama kana

> The plum tree
> Keeps its heart in tranquillity—
> See the green leaves!　　　　　(35)

These are smoothly flowing compositions on conventional themes in accordance with the canon as interpreted at Katsushika. Then lines like the following began to come from him.

> A runaway seeks sanctuary—
> But praises the white snow
> There's a man, indeed!　　　　　(36)

> All I saw
> Through the perspective glass
> —Threepenny worth of mist!　　　　　(37)

to which I would add from a later period:

> Birds build,
> Not knowing that the tree they choose
> Is the one to be felled!　　　　　(38)

It seems that his lectures did not please the orthodox of the school who complained to Mizoguchi Sogan, its head, and that Issa felt the strength of feeling against him and resigned to avoid less pleasant consequences after less than a year. About this time also he was haunted by a dream in which his father fell victim to malevolent influences in the household who caused some dreadful disaster. It impelled him to make his

(35) Ume no ki no kokoro shizuka ni aoba kana
(36) Nigekomu da shirayuki homeru danshi kana
(37) San-mon no kasumi mi ni keri engankyo
(38) Kiru ki to wa shirade ya tori no su wo tsukuru

26

first return to Kashiwabara. He left at the end of March 1791 and journeyed on foot to Kashiwabara, which he reached in the middle of May (the length of this journey contrasts oddly with those made later). He was overjoyed to find his father well and nothing untoward in the house.

> Tree by our gate
> Above all, you are unharmed—
> The evening cool! (39)

After a long talk about literary matters at Edo, Issa mentioned a plan he had for a tour through the western provinces and the southern islands of Shikoku and Kyushu. Such pilgrimages were frequently made at the time by literary and artistic notables, or would-be notables, and it was also customary for them to publish their travel journals containing essays, verses, sketches and the like. Apparently Yagobei encouraged his son's project and further justified it by mentioning a pilgrimage he himself had long wished to make to the great temple of Honganji in Kyoto in which he asked Issa to be his proxy.

So in the spring of the following year (1792) we find him taking leave of friends at Edo and of pupils, some of whom seem to have followed him from Katsushika.

> When shall we meet?
> I am for the far mists
> Where sea fires play. (40)

(39) Kado no ki mo mazu tsutsuganashi yu suzumi

(40) Itsu awan mi wa shiranuhi no to kasumi ('Shiranuhi', which I have translated here as 'sea fires', are will-o'-the-wisps which are common about Shimabara Bay, the western limit of Issa's journey. The word itself signifies 'unknown fires' and in the older poetry was the 'pillow-word' for the province of Chikugo or for Kyushu in general.)

He took the tonsure, as was not unusual for teachers at the time, and seems to have worn priestly costume thereafter. He also resigned the name Kikumei which he had inherited and as a mark of his new independence formally adopted the style Haikaiji Nyudo Issa-bo, which may be roughly interpreted 'Brother Issa, Lay Priest of the Temple of Poetry'.

> Here's the Spring
> And with it transmogrified
> Yataro becomes Issabo.   (41)

From the fact that his signatures, as Issa, resemble the flat spoon used in the tea ceremony it has been suggested that the name itself had some connection with that cult. But he himself tells us that it denotes a single bubble in a teacup which exists only for a moment, and this is consonant with the thoughts of impermanence which so often filled his mind rather than with his attitude towards any such elegant accomplishments. It is interesting to note that his friend Sarai (literally 'tea comes') also had a pen name connected with tea, and that Issa's lines have many fond references to the 'tea-mist' or the inviting steam which rises when tea is being made.

And so, with pilgrim's staff, straw sandals and broad sedge hat, Issa set out for the west along the Tokaido. His first journey was to last for some four years, but thereafter, so much was travel to his liking, he was to be frequently in the same costume, visiting friends and pupils, paying tribute at literary shrines, such as the tomb of Basho on the shore of Lake Biwa, and gathering materials to be used in prose and verse. We have

(41) Haru tatsuya Yataro aratame Issabo

a fairly close record of these years in journals which he pub-
lished afterwards and there is not space here to follow all his
wanderings as he saw for the first time Kyoto, the Inland Sea,
the craggy island of Shikoku and the rest. Some of the verses
he made on the road will be found in the second part of this
book; they are perhaps remarkable among those of the time
for the comparative paucity of literary and historical allusion.
After a visit to the shrines at Ise he travelled to Kyoto, where
he performed the observance his father had requested. He then
visited Osaka, Sakai and other points in the Kansai. Crossing
to Shikoku, he spent a short time in that island and then passed
on to Kyushu.

The New Year of 1793 he welcomed at a temple, the
Seikyoji, in the west of that island. Having thence called on
the poet Oryu at Kumamoto he proceeded to Nagasaki, where
he noted with only slight interest the strange appearance and
customs of foreigners.

> The Imperial Rule!
> Outlanders too are here
> At the secluded season.   (42)

The reference to the 'secluded season' shows that his mind was
still on Shinano, where the village would be already snow-
bound. Later he crossed again to Shikoku and spent some time
there. He stayed at the temple of Sennenji where the Abbot,
a priest named Gobai, was a close friend and appreciative
critic. He went in search of Sarai, the friend of his first days in
Edo, who had also become the chief priest of a temple, only
to find that he had been dead for some years.

(42) Kimi ga yo ya karahito mo kite toshi gomori

> Darkened our paths are and dreamlike,
> We tread them and lo! they are watery
> Ways of delusion! (43)

From his eagerness to maintain friendships and the ease with which he formed new ones through poetry with all conditions of men, we can assume that his developing nature remained simple and affectionate, whole-hearted in pursuit of his craft, modest as to his own accomplishment but anxious for the good opinion of those he respected, and most generous in praise of that of others. In Shikoku, as well as his priestly friends, he met a kindred spirit in Nijoan Chodo, a wealthy merchant of Matsuyama, who wrote verses. The two spent some time together and the following year Issa returned in December and stayed with him until the spring. At Osaka, whither Issa now returned, he renewed acquaintanceship with Oemaru, the old poet who had been a highway courier. Their relationship quickly ripened into friendship, for the robust strength and sanity of Oemaru expressed itself in his verse and was much to the taste of Issa. Furthermore, Oemaru showed himself in complete sympathy with Issa's revolt against the Katsushika school and their conventions. A farewell to Issa written when the latter, after a further prolonged stay, was finally leaving for Edo, appears in Oemaru's published verse.

> The wild geese yet
> Are content to stay—
> And must you return? (44)

Issa arrived back in Edo from his wandering in 1798—the

(43) Oboro oboro fumeba mizu nari mayoi michi
(44) Gan wa mada ochi tsuite iru nio kaeri ka

30

year of Wordsworth's *Lyrical Ballads*. The publication of his journals very soon attracted much attention. These, as well as *haiku*, contained a few *tanka*, some Chinese poems, and short prose essays written on places visited or incidents described to him. The great body of Issa's work is contained in this form. Some of the journals are numbered in an incomplete series, and others are called by the name of the 'era' during which they were compiled. Again there are in some laconic entries about the weather and the events of the day written above a varying number of *haiku* or *tanka* which are often repeated with minor revisions. They only occasionally refer to the incidents noted in the diary, but when they appear out of season—when, for instance, a *haiku* about the spring appears among autumn entries—they are marked with the name of that appropriate to them. Other markings show Issa as a persistent self-critic, always revising and amending, and selecting from these work-books verse for later collections, perhaps to have been like his book *Ora-ga-haru*, but which did not appear. Great events do not figure in the journals, even those like the peasant revolts near his own country and the eruptions of Asama, which might have been expected to concern him.

Shortly after his return to the capital, Issa formed a friendship with Natsume Seibi which was to remain to comfort and cheer him for the rest of his life. Seibi was a wealthy rice merchant—which then meant also financier—and something of a public figure. He was keenly interested in literature, particularly in *haiku*, and, writing verse himself, was possessed of a fine sense of form and a penetrating literary judgement on which Issa came to rely. The story of their meeting, while it may well have been invented, deserves at least mention here.

Issa had been kept waiting in the great man's outer office and when told that Seibi was after all engaged, got up to go, strewing on the floor the contents of a sack of *soba* flour he had brought as a present. With his foot he is said to have scrawled (although this is omitted from his collected works):

> Up in Shinano,
> There are Buddhas, there's the Moon,
> And there's our porridge! (45)

(*Soba*, of course, is not really like porridge, but in its implications here seems to correspond to it. '*Ora*' again is singular but has a tone of local pride and has been aptly likened by Mr Blyth to 'ma' for 'my' as heard in the Southern States; I would add the familiar 'ma' of 'ma mannie' heard in a northern one. The 'Buddhas' include pre-eminently the image at the imposing temple of Zenkoji and the moon is particularly celebrated for its beauty and the landscape it lights at Obasute-yama, also in Shinano.) When the verse was reported to Seibi he realised that he had to do with a man of worth as well as wit and he became Issa's friend and staunch admirer.

When thirty-nine, Issa visited Kashiwabara, and while he was at home his father had a serious attack of typhoid fever. Issa himself called the country physician from Nojiri. He held out little hope, but enjoined strict care and the avoidance of stimulants. Issa attended to the nursing for a month, but despite his vigilance his father was given wine and death soon followed. As the end approached, the old man tried to compose the quarrel between Issa and his stepbrother Senroku and started allocating some fields to Senroku, who however raised objections, assuming correctly that the main part of the

(45) Shinano de wa tsuki to hotoke to ora ga soba

32

property was to go to Issa. The father gave Issa a written document and made him promise to settle down and marry at Kashiwabara. This will the stepmother and Senroku afterwards refused to recognise and so baulked Issa of his inheritance for nearly thirteen years.

He could get little support from the village headman or other local authorities, perhaps because he had become for them, with his travel and his bookish ways, something of a stranger, whereas Senroku and his mother were respected and hard-working members of the community.

Issa chronicled the circumstances of his father's death in a pathetic short journal, called *Chichi no Shuen Nikki*. Our taste would condemn much of it, and indeed many of his other productions for being based on an overwrought and artificial sentimentality. Before turning away from them as altogether alien, however, it is as well to remember how Europe sighed over Werther's sorrows and how even robust eighteenth-century England piped its eye for Clarissa. More of the feeling Issa expressed on this and other occasions was true and universal than not, and the odd dress it assumes at times cannot completely hide its nature.

> If he were here, my father,
> We'd watch once again the day break
> Over green meadows. (46)

> The plum tree blossoms;
> The nightingale sings;
> But I am alone. (47)

(46) Chichi arite akebono mitashi aotabara
(47) Ume sakedo uguisu nakedo hitori kana

33

In Edo again he lodged for a time at Ueno, then lived at Atago, at Fukagawa and finally at Honjo. Pupils came to him readily as his reputation grew, he was on good terms with many of the eminent, Seibi remained his friend, and yet in these years his life was often one of poverty. This is the more mystifying when we learn that he carried almost to absurdity the frugality of his daily life and that visitors who called at his hut were frequently taken to dine at a restaurant where they had to pay for themselves. He enjoyed his untidy bachelor existence, however, and held aloof from anything like patronage or the fashions of the day. None the less, he accepted help in time of real need from his friends, and in 1809, when he lost his lodging, went to live for some months with Seibi at Asakusa. Many thousands were then homeless after a terrible fire which had devastated the city that New Year.

> The first of the year
> And I'm not the only one, eh?
> Bird without a nest. (48)

The story which Mr Bickerton recounts of his arrest, together with other guests, at Seibi's house on suspicion of stealing his friend's money, and their release only after prolonged examination and detention, is probably no more than a proof that Tokugawa justice was still swift, merciless and impartial.

There are a great many lines to bear witness to Issa's mischievous pleasure in his careless way of life in Edo, cleanliness and neatness being as much a social obligation as cravats and canes to the Regency buck.

(48) Ganjitsu ya ware nomi naranu su-nashi-dori

How agreeable it is,
My cotton gown—
Now it is soaked with sweat! (49)

Spiders in the corner—
Don't you be anxious,
I won't break your webs. (50)

There are also many anecdotes to tell of his offhand way and
lack of ceremony with the high-born and wealthy, usually
typified by Maeda, Lord of Kaga, whose retinue as a boy he
had watched with such awe. In most, Issa's behaviour may
strike us as churlish, but the extraordinary ceremony that then
surrounded the person of a daimyo must be remembered. On
one occasion, Kaga-no-Kami was passing through Kashi-
wabara and the village headman in a flutter appeared at Issa's
house to say that His Highness had commanded his presence.
Issa refused to go until the headman conceded that the com-
mand had actually been an invitation. He then proceeded to
the inn but, to the headman's consternation, in his oldest
clothes. To polite questions about his art he returned a sharp
answer condemning dilettantes and ended by saying that he
could not discuss its meaning with men of rank who treated
the art of poetry as a mere pastime. Undisturbed, the other
praised his work and presented him with several rolls of cloth.
These Issa carried home and threw on the midden, explaining
to his students that it might have seemed like affectation to
have refused the gift in the presence of the daimyo. On
another occasion he gave away a fine sandalwood writing-box
which Kaga-no-Kami had presented to him, because throngs

(49) Omoshiro ase no shimitaru yukata kana
(50) Sumi no kumo anjina susu wa toranu zoyo

of curious people came to see it. Throughout these incivilities it should be mentioned that the admiration he received from both this nobleman and others of rank appears to have been unshaken and that one of them contributed a preface to *Ora-ga-haru*.

During this later Edo period he made frequent efforts to make Senroku and his mother fulfil the terms of his father's will, but in vain. At last, after seven years had passed, his half-brother gave him a written undertaking that he would divide the property. Issa imprudently handed this document, together with the will itself, to the headman whom he had asked to act as arbitrator. Two years later nothing had been done, and Issa returned again to Kashiwabara to be confronted by further prevarication on Senroku's part and a flat denial by the head-man that he knew anything of the matter. To this occasion is attributed the well-known lines:

> Old village, my home,
> Everything I touch about you
> Turns to a thorn! (51)

In spite of this vexation, he continued to teach and made frequent tours about the country, often with pupils, some of whom he introduced to the beauties of Shinano. In May, 1810, he visited Kashiwabara but returned 'without changing his sandals'. However, his mind was now made up that Senroku must be brought to a settlement. He gradually wound up his affairs at Edo, announced that he was retiring to Shinano, and at the end of 1812, after a grand poetry party at Seibi's house where he composed more than one hundred *haiku*, actually did so, having taken lodgings at Kashiwabara.

(51) Furusato ya yoru mo sawaru mo bara no hana

He then let it be known that he was preparing a petition to the Shogun, since the property was on Tokugawa land. This was a tremendous and desperate step, likely to be as disastrous to the petitioner as to any other party, but also to bring ruin on any found to be at fault. The village was shocked and the Abbot of Myosenji, who had previously sought to bring about a compromise, again intervened—this time successfully. The property was equally divided between Issa and his stepbrother, even the house being partitioned by a wall down the middle.

> Is this it, then,
> My last resting place—
> Five feet of snow!   (52)

In the graveyard where he and his family are buried this verse is carved on an untrimmed stone which is his memorial. Issa sent it to Seibi for criticism with an alternative giving 'the place of my death' as the middle line, but Seibi pronounced in favour of the version that has survived. It has been assumed that Issa composed it when he came within sight of the village on his journey from Edo, and if this is true it is a witness to the strength of his determination.

Having at long last carried out one part of his father's injunction, he proceeded, with commendable promptitude, to the other, by which marriage had been enjoined on him. Early in 1814 he married Kiku, a farmer's daughter from the neighbouring hamlet of Akagawa, whose family were distantly related to his mother's. Kiku was a rosy, good-humoured lass of twenty-eight whose like is to be seen about the countryside to this day, dressed in the baggy blue and white trousers tight at the ankles, light-coloured kerchief and

(52) Kore ga maa tsui no sumika ka yuki goshaku

37

scarlet braids that still form their daily costume. Issa was sufficiently waggish about his late wooing.

> The love of deer!
> But as for people, I can tell you
> It can come at fifty! (53)

> Feet for a pillow
> And our arms intertwined—
> The tenderness of deer! (54)

Whatever were Kiku's feelings about her elderly husband, it is clear from the number and the nature of references to her in both journals and poems that she inspired him with deep affection. This is often expressed humorously, but as well as her own wholesome rustic charm she had the merit for him of being the first woman, since his mother, to give him the daily sympathy and steady companionship that can crown relations between the sexes after ardour has had its day.

> There's our Rose—
> A lot she cares, how she looks,
> How she goes! (55)

(*Kiku*, of course, is chrysanthemum, not rose, but as a girl's name in English life and poetry the connotations of the latter, I think, suggest more of what Issa intended.)

Despite this new preoccupation, he returned to Edo later in the year to take formal leave of the literary world at the capital. His reputation was now indeed unchallenged and his

(53) Hito naraba gojukurai zo shika no koi
(54) Ashi makura te makura shika no mutsumajiya
(55) Waga kiku ya nari ni mo furi nimo kamawazu ni

verses were widely copied. It was at last recognised that his strength and simplicity had brought something back to poetry lacking almost since Basho's death, and, if it was his quaint insect poems that first caught popular fancy, the grave elegiac music of others stayed longer in the listening mind.

> A wintered fly
> I freed and sent on its way—
> Grimalkin snatched!   (56)

> Heedless that the tolling bell
> Marks our own closing day—
> We take this evening's cool.   (57)

Not only in Edo but all over the country he became now a celebrated figure and in Shinano, and particularly on the route to Edo he had so often travelled, he had a host of friends and admirers. At Kashiwabara he was constantly being visited and much in demand as a teacher. It is characteristic that he preferred to call those who followed his guidance 'friends' rather than the more usual 'disciples'.

Again home at the end of the year, Issa celebrated his newly found happiness.

> Congratulation!
> Indeed it is for this—two people share
> The New Year bowl!   (58)

Some of the letters survive which Issa wrote to Kiku during his absences from home. They salute her with respect and

(56) Fuyu no hae wo nigaseba neko ni torarekeri
(57) Mi no ue no kane tomo shirade yusuzumi
(58) Medeto to iu mo futari no zoni kana

speak of his solicitude for her health and regret for the tedium to which he had left her. From Kashiwabara he continued to correspond with Seibi and to send him drafts for criticism.

Of the journals, the *Seventh Diary* (the numerical series is incomplete) is perhaps the most interesting as well as the most valuable, although it was not published until this present century had begun. It covers nine years of Issa's maturity as a poet which include his withdrawal from Edo, his marriage to Kiku, the short period of happiness which followed and the first of his later sorrows. An eminent critic has likened the poetry in it to the rounded fruit appearing which, in the preceding Bunka Verse Book (1808–1813), had often been hidden by the green leaves of high summer. The *Seventh Diary* was written in two parallel columns, the upper one having brief and often cryptic references to the weather and events of the day, the lower containing *haiku* written or revised at the time which sometimes but not often have reference to what is recorded above them. The biographer and student must often be disappointed by the diary entries. For instance, his marriage in April 1814 is chronicled thus:

    9th April—Cold as winter—to Ninokura
    10th ,, —Early morning hard frost—into the house
    11th ,, —Fair—wife came, Tokuzaemon stayed
    12th ,, —Fair
    13th ,, —Rain, townspeople came to offer congratu-
                lations—160 pence in.

(Tokuzaemon was the 'go-between' for the wedding. The money mentioned was doubtless made up of congratulatory presents.) On the other hand, a great number of verses at this time are playful conceits about the name Kiku, and even the

40

diary records his joy and anxiety when she told him that she was with child.

> The Chrysanthemum
> In her round straw hat—
> This morning's snow.   (59)

A son was born but lived only a month. In the following spring, while staying at a student's house, he dreamed—according to the diary—that Kiku had been delivered of another boy, and hurried home. Once again a dream had deceived him; a child was indeed born on the day he reached home but it turned out to be a girl. With their recent bereavement in mind the couple lavished all their care and affection on her, having given her the name of Sato, and Issa's description in *Ora-ga-haru* paints a charming little creature full of promise. Other entries in the diary about this time record correspondence with Seibi, laying down and finishing a stock of wine, dining with Kiku at the staging-inn as guest of the Nakamura family, and other happy occasions.

But much grief and misfortune was yet in store for Issa and his household. On Sato's second anniversary he wrote:

> Toddle and laugh!
> You're two years old, you know,
> This morning.   (60)

Less than six months later, she died after a sudden attack of small-pox. Issa and his wife were stunned by this blow and the poet's memories of Sato and the verses he wrote on this occasion are most moving. Among them is 'The world of dew

(59) O Kiku no sandara-boshi ya kesa no yuki
(60) Hae warae futatsu ni naru zo kesa kara wa

. . .' already quoted. Unhappily, another child, Ishitaro, born in 1820, the year after Sato's death, lived for only a few months.

> Haze in late spring shimmering—
> But what my eyes still follow
> Is that smiling face. (61)

Amid these bereavements Issa had written his *Eighth Journal* and *Ora-ga-haru*, a small book of verses, essays and sketches which many think contains his finest work. The matter of the essays and little anecdotes often seems thin, but we are told by those who are competent to judge that the style of it all is polished and charming. The *haiku* which follow the essays are serene in tone and have a kind of evening glow on them not of this world.

> After all, after all
> I commend myself and mine to you—
> Now at the year's end. (62)

(That is, to the Buddha.)

In the year of Ishitaro's death Issa was himself attacked by paralysis, which was thereafter to recur at intervals and obliged him to make his frequent journeys about the country-side on horseback. However, he accepted his recovery with gratitude, and evidently some surprise.

> This year and on
> All clear profit now for me—
> And here's the Spring! (63)

(61) Kagero ya me ni tsukimatou waraigao
(62) Tomokaku mo anata makase no toshi no kure
(63) Kotoshi kara marumoke zo yo kesa no haru

42

Kiku fell ill after the birth of another son. She had a long period of illness made more painful by arthritis and died in the spring of 1823. Issa had hurried to her bedside when her illness began and tended her with all his dearly bought experience of sickness. Perhaps it was because his love and sorrow were so deep that he wrote little about her death but mourned her even with a gentle smile.

> The moon tonight!
> If only she were here
> To hear my grumbles. (64)

I should not omit mention here of *haiga*, the rough impressionistic sketches which the *haiku* poets often attached to their verses. Issa did not leave a great number but they show some mastery of line and usually, some facet of his humour. The figure on the title page of this book is one of Issa's drawings, a self-portrait which is accompanied by the first *haiku* in the translations which follow. Another self-portrait, or rather self-cartoon, is better known in Japan and shows a very 'queer-looking figure' indeed with broad triangular head, lumpish nose, pouting lips and a receding chin. Appropriately enough it is accompanied by the lines.

> When seen
> Even by favouring eyes
> A queer-looking figure!
> (What people say about my looks—
>   people and Issa too!) (65)

It is of incidental interest that a bust of him which was carved

(64) Kogoto iu aite mo araba kyo no tsuki
(65) Hiiki me ni mite sae samui soburi kana

43

from the recollection of contemporaries shows nothing of this 'queerness' but a broad shouldered man with a wide humorous mouth and a nose of only moderate proportions.

A very well-known *haiku* which is thought to have been evoked by the sight of little Sato in the sunshine outside the house and intrigued by the hesitating flutter of a butterfly, runs:

> Garden butterfly
> The child crawls, it flutters,
> Crawls again, it flies. (66)

In a manuscript of which I have a tracing, this is written round an amusing sketch of a thatched hut and signed 'The house and Issa too'. My interpretation is that Issa wished to imply the household's delight in the spring sunshine and the charming scene and his own sympathy and part in it. This way of stressing his own place in the thoughts and feelings expressed in his verses—so diametrically opposed to classical principles —was almost a custom with him and I have given other examples elsewhere. It is as characteristic indeed as the phrase '. . . and Issa too'. Keats says somewhere in his letters:

'If a sparrow comes before my window I take part in its existence and pick about the gravel.'

Keats, we may add,—and Issa too!

The fourth son, Kinsaburo, died by reason of the carelessness of the woman employed to nurse him. She turned out to be the daughter of the village bully who had tormented Issa in childhood. To have a woman in the house, and perhaps an heir, Issa married again, in May 1824, Yuki, a lady of *samurai*

(66) Niwa no cho ko ga haeba tobi haeba tobu

44

family. But neither the house nor the bridegroom were to her liking, and she left him after only a few weeks for her father's house. As she gave no sign of returning, Issa sent a bill of divorce to her in August with the wry comment,

> If you've severed it,
> The vine of the gourd plant—
> Throw it back in the water! (67)

The same month, he was taken ill at Zenkoji with a form of paralysis which made speech difficult, and stayed for treatment at the house of a pupil in that city, who was also a physician.

For his New Year verse in 1823 he had written:

> Here's the New Year
> And on top of old foolishness
> New folly is piled. (68)

For 1825, being sixty-three, he wrote:

> Land of the Gods!
> Without fail the grasses bud
> Even on New Year's day. (69)

—a strange observation for snowbound Shinano, but perhaps he was thinking of some cherished pot-plant.

This year he married yet again, choosing more wisely a woman from Echigo named Yao, who had worked for some time in the district as a wet nurse. His compositions during this and the preceding years are contained in the *Eighth Diary*.

In the summer of 1827 there was a destructive fire at

(67) Hechima tsuru kitte shimaeba moto no mizu
(68) Haru tatsu ya gu no ue ni mata gu ni kaeru
(69) Shinkoku ya kusa mo ganjitsu kitto saku

Kashiwabara during which the house that had been the subject of such bitter debate was destroyed. Pupils and friends invited Issa and his wife to stay with them, but he declined and the couple lived in the narrow storehouse, without window or chimney, which is still shown as his last dwelling-place. Later in the year he became bedridden but recovered, so that by November he was able again to visit pupils and friends on foot. However, on the 19th of that month after a walk in the snow the paralysis returned and he died suddenly and apparently without pain at the age of sixty-five. A persistent tradition states that he recited the following farewell *haiku* which indeed is not out of character:

> Tub to tub
> The whole journey—
> Just Hub-bub! (70)

(That is, from the baby's first bath to the washing of the body.)

Another interpretation is that Issa is deprecating the gibberish which he says he has uttered all his life.

However, one of the Nakamura family tells us that death when it came allowed no time for any spoken valediction and that the following verse which I have already quoted was found under his pillow. It must therefore be called his last poem.

> A blessing indeed—
> This snow on the bed-quilt,
> This, too, is from the Pure Land. (71)

He was buried among the family graves on the little hill of

(70) Tarai kara tarai ni utsuru chimpunkan
(71) Arigata ya fusuma no yuki mo Jodo yori

Komaruyama where the modest monument now stands, bearing his acceptance of a 'last resting place, five feet of snow'.

The following spring, his posthumous daughter, Yata, was born, the only child who survived him. Through her his line has been maintained and the property to this day remains in the hands of his descendants. His verses and other writings were collected and published by pupils and admirers, although some, like the *Seventh Diary*, had to wait until much later and this naturally delayed full appreciation of his work. But he has always been admired and loved in his own country of Nagano, and at Kashiwabara itself his memory is venerated and his relics preserved with a zeal and affection that surpass any literary cult. Only at Alloway have I seen anything like it, and because Kashiwabara is more remote it has been able to avoid some of Alloway's excesses.

The translations which follow are, with some few exceptions, arranged in chronological order. I have been at pains to limit the notes to factual matters which seem to call for explanation and to avoid further comment on Issa's qualities, which I hope will make themselves felt, however imperfectly, through some of the English versions. However, I would end with a short quotation from his essay, *Exhortation to the Farmers*,* in which some, like Professor Yamato, may hear something of Hesiod or Virgil, and others a reminder of Johnson's sonorous 'Pour forth thy fervours for a healthful mind'. We may smile at such an earnest call to the fields as this coming from one who had never worked in them himself since boyhood, and

*This is not now thought to be by Issa but the fact that it was for long attributed to him strongly suggests that it does in fact represent what was known to be his attitude of mind.

who had thus waggishly confessed himself an idler.

> People of the Fields
> From my heart I bow to you!   (72)
> —Now for a noontide nap.

But, as Mr Blyth has said so well in his *Haiku* (Volume I, p. 344), the Exhortation has a higher purpose than to reconcile farmers to a life of toil. 'Life is more important than art' (so Mr Blyth reads the message), 'but art and poetry are to be put into our living. Beauty is to be found in our daily life; it is then created naturally and spontaneously.'

   This is how Issa's essay begins: 'Desire the raising of crops in the fields about your house rather than the planning of flower gardens to pleasure the eye. Take a hoe in your own hand and use it. Preserve with all care what you received from forebears; cherish with all affection your parents as long as they live. Rather than the cherry flowers of Yoshino or the moon at Sarashina, enjoy whatever the work is you may have to do. Morning and evening still your heart. . . .'

(72) No no hito wo kokoro kara ogamu hirune kana

POEMS

I · Mostly of Place

1

Ora ga yo ya	This world of ours!
Sokora no kusa mo	Even the grasses over there
Mochi ni naru	Give us our gruel.

This verse accompanies the self-portrait which appears on the title page. By way of comment, Issa adds in prose 'It is for courtiers and the like to mourn the waning of the moon and to sing the praises of blossoms.'

2

Nagai zo yo	The night is long indeed,
Yo ga nagai zo yo	Know it is very long!
Namu Amida	Praise to Lord Buddha!

Amida is the Buddha of the Western Paradise, whose best-known statue in Japan is the Great Buddha at Kamakura.

3   *Of a Cripple Entering the Zenkoji*

Kagero ya	Through springtime haze
Te ni geta haite	Wearing sandals on his hands
Zenkoji	He enters Zenkoji.

The Zenkoji, which figures much in Issa's verse, is an imposing Buddhist temple at Nagano, the city near his birthplace. For centuries it has been venerated throughout Japan and a proverb associated with it—'led by a cow to the Zenkoji' has been woven by Issa into the following *haiku*.

4

Harukaze ya	The spring wind!
Ushi ni hikarete	Drawn by a cow
Zenkoji	To visit Zenkoji.

Legend tells of an irreligious old woman who had set out strips of cloth to dry. One was snatched up by a sportive cow which, on being pursued by the old woman, led her into the precincts of the temple. The Buddha appeared, softened her heart, and restored her washing to her when she returned home. The saying is therefore applied to good coming out of an apparent mischance.

5

Meigetsu ya	O radiant moon!
Nishi ni mukaeba	If you look to the west you'll see
Zenkoji	Zenkoji

6

Of a Beggar before the Zenkoji

Jubako no	In his box
Zeni shigomon ya	Four or five coppers, and now
Yushigure	The evening drizzle!

7

Yukeburi mo	With this night of moonlight
Tsukiyo no haru to	And the vapours from my bath ...
Nari ni keri	Spring has begun!

8

At Hakone

Nadeshiko ya	The wild pinks in flower
Jizo Bosatsu no	All about the Holy Jizo.
Ato-saki ni	

The *nadeshiko*, or wild pink, is sometimes employed, for its grace and gentle charm, as an emblem of ideal womanhood, while its name is written with the characters, 'to comfort' and 'child'. Jizo is the Buddhist deity who helps all in trouble, but he is pre-eminently the patron of children, pregnant women, and travellers. His images are very often found at cross-roads and are frequently heaped about with pebbles with which he helps the souls of young children to accomplish the toils set them in purgatory.

9

Nomidomo ga	For you fleas too,
Yonaga daro zo	The night may be long perhaps
Samishikaro	And is it not lonely!

10

Akikaze ya	Ah, the autumn wind!
Are mo mukashi no	He and that likely lad
Bishonen	Of long, long ago!

11

Waga hotoke	My departed one!
Kyo mo izuku no	Where has it been set tonight
Kusa makura	Your grassy pillow.

'Pillow of grass' is a common figure of speech for travel, as the 'autumn wind', with a slightly more literary air, was for man's mortality.

12

Meigetsu ya	Radiant moon!
Kyo wa anata mo	Tonight, must you too
On isogi	Hasten thither?

13

Furu inu ya	Our old dog,
Mimizu no uta ni	Looking as if he hears them with interest,
Kanji-gao	The canticles of worms.

14

Mushi naku na	Cry not, insects,
Soko wa shonin no	For that is a way
Hairiguchi	We all must go.

15

Yamabuki ya	The yamabuki
Kusa ni kakurete	Hidden by the grasses—
Mata soyogu.	And then again they sway.

The yamabuki, *Kerria japonica*, is a plant with a yellow rose-like flower.

16

Meigetsu wa	The bright moon—
Shio ni nagaruru	And a little boat comes drifting
Kobune kana	Drifting down the tide.

17

Yugure ya	Evening—
Ike naki kata mo	And the cherry blossoms are falling
Sakura chiru	Where there is no pond, also.

18

Waga haru wa	My Spring?
Take ippon ni	A single bamboo—
Yanagi kana	A willow twig.

Although associated with many ideas similar to those of our own season, the spring for Japanese of Issa's day began with the New Year. Here it is the New Year decoration, a part of which developed into the *kadomatsu*, to which he refers. Most houses now have a pair of *kadomatsu*, consisting of pine and bamboo formally arranged, set before the porch.

19

Kumo no mine	Peak in the clouds!
Mikoshi mikoshite	We watch and watch to see it show
Aso kemuri	Through Aso's smoke.

The massive volcano of Aso-san in Kyushu, which is still active, has five separate peaks.

20

Mikagirishi	Long I had left it—
Furusato no	And still at the old village
Sakura saki ni keri	Cherry trees burgeoned.

21

No daiko mo　　　　　The wild turnip was in flower
Hana saki ni keri　　And the skylark singing.
Naku hibari

22

Kaminari ni　　　　　Resoundingly
Naki-awasetaru　　　The thunder rumbled
Kigisu kana　　　　　And the pheasants at once
　　　　　　　　　　　Cheeped all together.

23

Onna kara saki e　　Twilight spreads
Kasumu zo　　　　　From the woman waiting on
　　　　　　　　　　　the shore
Shiohigata　　　　　Over the evening tide.

24　　　　　　　*On Arriving at Edo*

Kasa no hae　　　　Fly on my hat
Mo kyo kara wa　　Today, you know,
Edo mono zo　　　　You're an Edokko!

25

Yare utsu na　　　　Spare the Fly!
Hae ga te wo suri　Wringing his hands, wringing
　　　　　　　　　　　his feet,
Ashi wo suru　　　　He implores your mercy!

26

Suzume ko mo
Ume ni kuchi aku

Nebutsu kana

The little sparrows
They open their mouths at the
plum tree—
This too is worship!

27

Furu ame ni
Hitori nokori shi
Hana no kage

Plump falls the rain—
And only one man is left
Beneath the cherry flowers.

28

Furusato no
Mienaku narite
Naku hibari

My village—
Out of sight it is and yet
The lark is singing there.

29

Sumire saku
Kado ya yoru sae
Natsukashiki

The gate where Violets show,
In memory, how it is loved—
Even when night has fallen.

30

Waga mae ni
Dare dare sumi shi

Sumire zo mo ·

Before I came
Who and who was dwelling
here?
Violets remained.

31

Kari naku ya	Here make your cry,
Heike jibun no	Wild Geese! . . . The house on the shore
Hama no iye	Stood from the Taira's day.

The Taira were the warrior house who held the supreme power in Japan for a brief period in the twelfth-century until it was wrested from them by their rivals, the Minamoto.

32

Waga hoshi wa	My star—
Kazusa no sora wo	Does it hover yet I wonder
Urotsuku ka	In the Kazusa sky?

Kazusa was one of the provinces—replaced now by the prefectures—and lay to the east of Tokyo Bay facing the city of Edo.

33

Aki no kaze	Winds of autumn—
Tsurugi no yama wo	Is it the Hill of Falchions
Kuru kaze ka	Whence you come?

Tsurugi—the word itself signifies a sword of antique design—is the name of one of the three summits of Hakusan, a mountain to the west of Nagano. '*Tsurugi no yama*' sometimes means a place of torment while 'To scale the hill of swords' is sometimes used to denote the performance of a hazardous feat.

34

Aki no kaze	Winds of autumn—
Ware wa mairu wa	The one I'm travelling to,
Dono jigoku	Which hell is it?

At a temple after seeing pictures of hells and purgatories which the religious art of Japan has depicted in colours no less lurid than those of the West.

35

Aki no kaze	Winds of autumn—
Kojiki wa ware wo	And a beggar eyes me
Mi-kuraburu	Appraisingly!

'Appraisingly' by comparison with himself rather than as a calculation of probable alms.

36

Asa samu ya	O the morning cold!
Matsu wa kyonen no	But the pine tree is the pine tree
Matsu naredo	Of last year.

37

Kirigirisu	Cricket!
Tonari ni ite mo	Although it was next door you sang—
Kikoekeri	I heard you here.

38

Shiragiku ni	White chrysanthemums!
Tsutanaki chozu	They've pitched water on you
Kakaru nari	From the washing bowl.

39

Ware ue shi
Matsu mo oikeri
Aki no kure

It has aged indeed
The pine tree that I planted—
Now autumn's ending!

40

Yuri saku ya
O hone otte
Hibari naku

The lily flowered—
And, after much travailing
The skylark sang!

41

Nani goto mo
Tanomi nakereba
Namu Amida

What's this?
Not a thing he's asking for—
Yet praises the Buddha!

42

Yo nashi wa

Ware to mugura zo
Hototogisu

We've no special business
cuckoo,
I and the burweed now,
O Bird of Time.

43

Ware nanji wo
Matsu koto hisashi
Hototogisu

A long, long wait
I've had for you here—
O Cuckoo, Bird of Time!

Issa's note shows that this refers to the story of the encounter on a bridge of Chang Liang with a sage whose sandal had fallen into the river. When Chang retrieved it, the Elder appointed a meeting five days later at the same bridge when he would be rewarded. Chang arrived exactly at the time named, according to some versions of the story, a little late according to others, and the sage reproved him for unpunctuality. This happened several times until Chang respectfully presented himself before the other's arrival. He was then given a scroll with the statement 'Who studies this will give instruction to Kings'. It contained an exposition of the Art of War and Chang became counsellor to Kao Tsu, assisting him to gain the Imperial power as first of the Han dynasty.

44

Hito wa	Up start the snipe!
Toshitoru beki mono zo	Men must take the years that come
Shigi no tatsu	Know they are thus!

45

Yuki saki mo	Whither does he make his way?
Tada akikaze zo	Only where the autumn winds blow
Kojunrei	The little pilgrim!

Verses of the Pilgrimage

46

Kamakura ya	At Kamakura—
Mukashi donata no	Whose were you in the olden time
Chiyo tsubaki	Aged camellia?

Kamakura, as an old military stronghold and capital, has numerous associations with history and romance.

47

Kasa sashite	Umbrellas at the ready,
Hakone kosu nari	We crossed the Hakone passes
Haru no ame	In the spring rain.

48

Oigawa miete	The Oigawa in sight—
Sore kara	And look, look over there,
Hibari kana	A skylark rises!

The Oigawa, between Shizuoka and Nagoya, has a wide bed of pebbles, much broader than its stream, which is seen at a considerable distance from the surrounding high ground. The current being too swift for ferry boats, in Issa's time travellers were carried across on wooden platforms by large gangs of coolies.

49

Hamamatsu ya	At Hamamatsu—
Semi ni yorube no	The wave voices accompany
Nami no koe	Cicadas.

Hamamatsu, an old castle town on the Tokaido, is at a point where the highway approaches the ocean.

50   *At Lake Biwa*

Kame dono no	Master Tortoise, now,
Ikutsu no toshi zo	How many years would his be pray?
Fuji no yama	Peerless Mount Fuji.

Biwa is a large lake near Kyoto, much celebrated in art and literature. It is characteristic that Issa avoids 'poetising' and the 'Eight Beauties of Biwa' in such surroundings.

51

Gichuji e	The first drizzle
Isogi soro	Just as we were making all speed
Hatsu shigure	For Gichuji.

At this temple, dedicated to the doughty and ill-fated warrior of the Minamoto, Yoshinaka, the great poet Basho chose to be buried. It is in a position of much beauty on the shore of Lake Biwa, and Issa has many verses to show that he not only visited it but that it was frequently in his thoughts. He attended a memorial service for Basho there in 1795.

52   *At the Grand Shrines of Ise*

Onozukara	Of itself
Atama ga sagaru	The head bows in reverence
Kamijiyama	At Kamijiyama.

The Ise shrines, dedicated to the high deities, Amaterasu-Omikami and Toyo-uke-Omikami, are the most important in the Shinto faith, and in Issa's time as in ours were the subject of thousands of pilgrimages. Although many of them were no more solemn than that of the Wyf of Bath, visitors without any reverence for Shinto have often remarked on the atmosphere of peaceful sanctity that seems to surround the place, in part created by tradition, in part by the plain wooden buildings set in surroundings of unusual loveliness. Kamijiyama is a hill within the precincts, the name of which signifies literally 'The Way of the Gods' as does the word Shinto itself.

53

Hakidame e	The Crane comes down
Tsuru no sagarikeri	Right on the rubbish heap
Waka-no-Ura	At Waka-no-Ura

There is a well-known *tanka* by Akahito, the famous eighth-century poet, in which he writes of the cranes flying at flood tide over the wide bay of Waka-no-Ura and, finding no dry land to alight on, flocking on towards the reeds at the shore. 'Crane on a rubbish heap' is a common figure of speech, equivalent to something like 'pure gold in dross'.

54

Jigoku e wa	Thus sings cuckoo—
Ko maire to ya	This way down, this way to hell
Kankodori	At Koyasan.

The great monastery of Kongo-buji on Koyasan founded by the eminent Kobo Daishi has, among many other monuments, one statue called the Perspiring Jizo. It is so named because it is believed to bear the traces every morning of the sufferings undergone by the benevolent Jizo in hell to relieve those condemned to its tortures.

55   *At Nara*

Daibutsu no	Sallying out
Hana kara detaru	From the nose of the Buddha
Tsubame kana	Darts a swallow.

The Great Buddha at Nara, which is a representation of Roshana, was completed in A.D. 750, but the present head was added some eight centuries later to replace one lost by fire. The face is black and grotesque with wide nostrils.

56

Hana saku ya	So the flowers bloom—
Kyo no bijin no	But look at their insouciance
Hokaburi	The belles of the capital!

'*Hokaburi*', here attributed to the women of Kyoto, who have always been noted for accomplishments and their not uncalculated charm, is a kind of secular 'know-nothingness' of which the symbol, often seen on the stage, is a coif-like napkin worn over the head.

57   *At the Honganji*

Suzushisa ya   The coolness!
Amida Jobutsu no   In such a blessed place indeed
Kono Kata wa   Amida would become a Buddha.

The Honganji (Temple of the Original Vow) is the magnificently imposing temple at Kyoto at which Issa carried out certain observances on his father's behalf. It is dedicated to Amida, whose original vow it was that he would not become a Buddha, unless salvation could be attained by all who sincerely desired it.

58   *At Osaka*

Fune ga tsuite   'Sir—an it please you
Soro to hagu   The boat is at hand'—
Futon kana   Off with the quilts!

59   *At Akamagaseki*

Meigetsu ya   A famous moon!
Kami mo   Tonight the Crabs even
Taira wo nanorideru   Proclaim their Taira birth.

In the year 1185 at the great sea-fight of Dan-no-Ura, the forces of the Taira, who had hitherto been all-powerful, were finally overthrown by the Minamoto under their brilliant young leader

Yoshitsune. It was said that some of the angry souls of the defeated Taira warriors passed into crabs, a kind of which, peculiar to the neighbourhood, has on the shell markings which suggest the be-whiskered and helmeted face of a medieval warrior. Akama is on the seaward side of the Straits of Shimonoseki, opposite the bay where the main battle was joined.

60

Suzukaze ya
Chikara ippai
Kirigirisu

There's a cool breeze!
Now, Grasshoppers, sing,
Sing with all your might!

61

Natsuyama ya
Hitori kigen no

Ominaeshi

On the hill of summer
Stands the slender maiden
flower
In a solitary humour.

62

Suzushisa ya
Yama kara mieru
Ozashiki

From the hill
How cool it looks—
The spacious room.

63

Suzukaze wa
Anata makase zo

Haka no matsu

The cool breezes!
Trust we to the Grace that
sends them,
Pine tree at the tomb.

64

Akatombo
Kare mo yube ga

Suki ja yara

Red dragon-fly—
He's one too that likes the even-
ing,
Or so it seems.

65

Tsuyu no yo no
Tsuyu no naka nite
Kenka kana

A world of dew!
And even in that dewdrop—
Altercation!

66

Tsuyu chiru ya
Gosho daiji ni

Naku suzume

The dews dissolve;
With reverence do your office
    now,
Chirping sparrow!

67

Furusato ya
Chisai ga ore ga
Natsu kodachi

At our village
There's a summer shaw—
Mine it is though small.

68

Shogatsu ya
Yoso ni saite mo
Ume no hana

January it is—
But in other provinces
The plum has bloomed already.

69

O ame ya
Tsukimi no fune mo

Miete furu

A great downpour,
And the moon-viewing party's
    boat
Appears—and the rain falls!

70

Medetasa wa
Kazusa no ka ni mo
Kuwarekeri

Here's luck indeed!
Bitten by the mosquitoes
Of Kazusa too!

71

Hikoboshi no   Smiling pleasantly,
Nikoniko miyuru   There between the trees
Ko no ma kana   Shines the Herdsman Star!

This, and the next two verses, refer to Tanabata, or the Festival of the Weaving Lady, which on the seventh day of the seventh month celebrates her yearly meeting with the Herdsman, her earth-born lover. As the star we know as Vega, she is condemned for her indiscretion to sit at her loom on one side of the River of Heaven, or Milky Way, while he, whom we call Altair, keeps his herds on the other.

72

Shan shan to   Clap! clap! go the looms—
Mushi mo hata orite   Insects, you weave too
Hoshi mukae   And welcome the Stars.

73

Naku na mushi   Cry not, small Insects!
Wakaruru koi wa   Even the Stars above
Hoshi ni sae   Part from their lovers.

This was written at Tanabata in 1822 when his cherished wife, Kiku, lay ill of the sickness from which shortly afterwards she was to die.

74

Tsuyu no tama   Pearls of the dew!
Hitotsu hitotsu ni   In every single one of them
Furusato ari   I see my home.

75

Waga inu ga	Look at our Dog!—
Tonbo-gaeri no	Turns a back-somersault—
Hana no kana	Must be the blossom!

76

Meigetsu ya	The radiant moon!
Hotoke no yo ni	Like a Buddha I sit,
Hiza wo kumi	Knees drawn up.

77

Korogi wa	A Cricket, is it?
Shimoyo no koe wo	This night of frost
Jiman kana	With such a vaunting voice.

Two manuscripts show this verse accompanied by *haiga*. One is a fan bearing a self-portrait in the manner of the cover decoration; the other includes a rather careful drawing of a cock with head on one side, as if listening to a challenge.

78

Yuki tokete	The snow thaws—
Mura ippai no	And suddenly the whole village
Kodomo kana	Is full of children!

79

Suzume no ko	Fledgling sparrows
Jizo no sode ni	They are sheltering there
Kakurekeri	In Jizo's sleeve.

80

Tori nado mo	To birds and others too,
Koi wo seyo tote	'Take your love now' they seem to say,
Yakuno kana	These burning fields.

Written in the month before he married Kiku.

81

Kimi ga yo wa	Our Imperial Land!
Kon no noren mo	For shop-front aprons also
Sakura kana	There are Cherry Flowers.

'*Kimi ga yo*'—the first words now of Japan's anthem—is properly of the Imperial Line, rather than the land, but Issa often seems to use it, as here, to sing the blessings of his country. The '*noren*' is a short divided curtain, usually of the same blue as a butcher's apron, which hangs across a shop entrance and bears the owner's name or an allusion to his wares in decorative script.

82

Ippon no kusa mo	Within this single stalk of grass
Suzukaze	The cool wind has lodged.
Yadorikeri	

83

Neta inu ni	In sleep
Fuwa to kabusaru	The dog is lightly coroneted
Hito ha kana	By a paulownia leaf.

84

Tsuyu chiru ya   The dews dissolve—
Jigoku no tane wo   And seeds of hell are sown
                          again
Kyo mo maku   Again today.

85

Yo ni tsurete   As the world goes—
Hanabi no tama mo   The jewels of the fireworks
                          show
Okii zo   Prodigious they are.

Written while he was in Edo to receive the plaudits and farewells of
the 'literary world'.

86

Kyo no hi ya   This day of all days,
Shinano sodachi mo   What we've raised in Shinano
Kiku no hana   Is a Chrysanthemum.

This appears in the *Seventh Journal* four months after his marriage to
O Kiku.

87

Motaina ya   Disquieting it is
Hirune shite kiku   While I am at my noonday nap
Taue-uta   To hear the planting song!

88

Hotarumi ya   Firefly-viewing . . .
Korobinagara mo   And just as one stumbles—
Are hotaru   Look, there's a firefly!

89

Yugao ya	There blow the moon flowers
Uma no shiri e mo	And one has just blossomed
Hitotsu saku	By Dobbin's buttocks!

90

Hito no yo ni	The world of men—
Ta ni tsukuraruru	But in its miry paddy fields
Hasu no hana	The Lotus is fashioned.

91

Yo no naka ya	Through this world of ours
Cho no kurashi mo	The butterfly's existence—
Isogashiki	Such a hastening!

92

Sakura mite	Seeing the cherry flowers—
Aruku aida mo	And even when we're strolling thus
Kogoto kana	Grumbles are heard!

93   *At Negishi*

Yamabuki wo	The rustic fence
Sashidashi kao no	Seems to be offering us
Kakine kana	A Kerria flower.

Probably a reference to the well-known tale of Ota Dokan, the fifteenth-century baron who first fortified Edo. While hawking near Totsuka he was caught by a shower and, reining up before a farmstead, called for a straw cape. After a pause a girl appeared, silently handed Ota a spray of kerria and re-entered the cottage. He was not unnaturally irritated at this seeming discourtesy. However, a retainer explained the girl's action as a poetical way of expressing regret that no cape was at hand, based on a punning allusion to an old poem, and Ota, ashamed of his ignorance, forthwith became an eager student of literature.

94   *At the Old Capital*

Iza na nore	Come, before the noble pine,
Matsu no gozen zo	Declare your name and style,
Hototogisu	Cuckoo!

95

Suzukaze mo	The cooling breeze—
Hotoke makase no	And I resigning to the Buddha
Wagami kana	This soul of mine.

96

Waga io wa	Round my hermitage
Kusa mo natsuyase	The grasses too have known it—
Shitarikeri	Summer faintness!

97

Kore wa sate	Listen! O listen!
Nemimi ni mizu no	Like water into sleeping ears
Hototogisu	The cuckoo's song.

98

Nete okite	Sleeping, waking,
O akubi shite	Giving such tremendous yawns—
Neko no koi	The cat goes courting!

99

Sakura sakura	O cherry, cherry!
To utawareshi	So was it praised in song,
Oi ki kana	This venerable tree.

100

Meigetsu ya	A radiant moon—
Taka Kannon no	And we are at the blessed knees
O hiza moto	Of our Lady Kannon.

Kannon, or Avalokitesvara, is a Buddhist personification of compassion, masculine in other times and places but feminine in Japan. Her name has been interpreted as 'She who pauses with her foot upon the threshold of Heaven to listen to the cry of distress from earth'.

101

Akai tsuki	Red moon—
Kore wa tare no ja	Now whose is that
Kodomotachi	Children?

102

Yamaudo wa	There's the highlander
Kura wo makura ya	With his mattock as a pillow!
Naku hibari	And the skylark sings!

103

Yo no naka wa
Jigoku no ue no
Hanami kana

In the world's way—
On the roof of hell we walk
Gazing at flowers!

104

Sore de koso
On hotogisu
Matsu no tsuki

That's it, of course!
To pine trees and the moon
Add the honourable cuckoo!

105

Ware shinaba
Hakamori to nare
Kirigirisu

And, when I die,
Be thou guardian of my tomb,
Grasshopper.

106

Furu-inu ga
Saki ni tatsu nari
Haka-mairi

Visiting family graves,
The lead is taken there in front
By our aged Dog.

107

Shitaya
Ichiban no kao shite
Koromogae

In Shitaya
He cuts the smartest figure now
With the change of clothes.

On the first day of the fourth month, a convention of Issa's time required almost everybody in Old Japan to appear in new, or at least lighter, clothes. The lines are a waggish reference to his own habit of dress in which he affected extreme carelessness, no doubt to outrage the Edo dandies who set great store by those respectable fetishes, neatness and cleanliness.

108

Mijikayo ya
Yo ya to iu koso
Hito mo hana
(Hito mo Issa)

The night of summer!
How brief it is, how brief it is
So say men at prime.
(Men—and Issa too.)

109

Uguisu yo
Edo no himuro wa
Nani ga saku

Ah, Nightingale!
In the ice-rooms of Edo
What's now in bloom?

The *uguisu*, more properly bush-warbler, is usually mentioned by Issa with admiration. However, the cultivation of their voices had become a fashionable craze and at one time two wardens were appointed to Ueno to guard the birds taken under the august patronage of the Shogun, and to eradicate if possible deplorable traces of Eastern dialect which had appeared in their songs!

110

Hatsuzemi to
Ieba shoben
Shitarikeri

'That's the first cicada'
He observed—and then
   Piddled!

111

Mikazuki to
Sori ga au yara

Hototogisu

The crescent moon!
How it seems to meet your mood—
Cuckoo!

112

Kimi ga yo wa	Our Imperial Land!
Onna mo sunari	An ardent woman—
Fuyu gomori	And winter seclusion!

113

Naku na kari	Wild Geese, hush your cry!
Dokko mo onaji	Wherever you go it is the same—
Ukiyo zo ya	The Floating World!

114

Nana-korobi	The maiden flower—
Ya-oki no hana yo	Seven times down, eight times up—
Ominaeshi	That's her quality!

115

Uguisu ya	The Nightingale
Doroashi nuguu	On the petals of the Plum—
Ume no hana	Wipes her muddy feet!

116

Inu no ko no	Under the willow
Kuwaete netaru	With a leaf stuck in his mouth
Yanagi kana	The puppy sleeps.

117

Yo kagura ya	By night sacred music
Takibi no naka e	And into the flare of the torches
Chiru momiji	Float crimson leaves!

The *kagura* is a stately dance performed at Shinto shrines to the sound of flute and drum.

118

Ku no shaba ya	A world of care!
Sakura ga sakeba	And if the Cherry flowers—
Saita tote	Well; it has flowered!
	(Men—and Issa too)

119

U no hana ya	There's the Hare-blossom—
Kami to kojiki no	Between God and the Beggar
Naka ni saku	It has bloomed.

'Hare blossom' is *Deutzia crenata*, and the 'maiden flower' of No. 114 is *Patrinia*, a flower with many tender connotations in Eastern literature.

III · Mostly in Retirement

120   *Of his retirement*

Kakurega ya   The tucked away cottage—
Ha no nai kuchi de   No teeth in the mouth now,
Fuku wa uchi   But, luck's in the house!

'*Fuku wa uchi*' is the cry raised at the 'bean scattering' festival of Setsubun, the other half being '*Oni ga soto*'—'Demons! out with you!'

121

Shinanoji ya   In our Shinano
Yuki ga kiereba   Soon as the snow has thawed
Ka ga sawagu   The Gnats start their fuss!

122

Harusame ya   Spring rain—
Kuware nokori no   And the Ducks who were not
                               eaten
Kamo ga naku   Acclaim it with song!

123

O neko yo   Off with you!
Hayaku ike ike   Off with you! Great Cat,
Tsuma ga naku   There's your wife a-bawling!

124

Waga yado ya   At my lodging
Nezumi to naka no   The Fireflies are on good terms
Yoi hotaru   With the Mouse.

78

125

Shogatsu ya　　　　January's here—
Ume no kawari no　　And instead of plum blossoms
O fubuki　　　　　　A flurry of snow!

126

Damare semi　　　　Silence, Cicada!
Ima hige dono ga　　The Lord Whiskers in person
Gozaru zo yo　　　　Is now at hand.

127

Saki no yo no　　　　In another world
Ore ga itoko ka　　　Was I perhaps your cousin
Kankodori　　　　　　Cuckoo?

128

Nomi no ato　　　　　Flea-bites!
Sore mo wakaki wa　　They too thanks to her youth
Utsukushiki　　　　　Are beautiful!

129

Geta karari　　　　　Clogs going clip—clopper—
Karari yonaga no　　What an endless night
Yatsura kana　　　　They make of it!

130

Usosamu ya　　　　　A little chill it grew,
Oya to iu ji wo　　　As we learned at last the mean-
　　　　　　　　　　　　ing
Shitte kara　　　　　Of the word 'parent'.

131

Kiku saku ya   A Chrysanthemum flowers—
Maguso yama mo   And with that pile of dung as
                        setting—
Hito-keshiki   There's a scene for you!

132   *At the Inn*

Saru hito ga   The Guest departed,
Manmaru ni neru   One who slept wrapped like a
                        ball—
Futon kana   Look at the quilts!

133

Tada tanome   Trust, only trust!
Tanome to tsuyu no   And trust again—thus it is
Koborekeri   The dew comes down!

134

Yoi yo ja to   The good world that it is!
Tsuyu ga zanburi   Thus the dew, as it plashes,
Zanburi kana   Plashes gently down.

135

Ariake ya   Day breaks—
Ume ni mo hitotsu   And even by the plum tree
Hachi tataki   One beats his bowl!

Tsuma-goi ya	Seeking a wife—
Hisoka wakai	But no young stag it is that comes
Shika de nashi	Thus stealthily!

Written a few months after his own wooing.

137

Ogiku ya	Such a Chrysanthemum!
Makeru soburi wa	She never looked once as if
Nakari shi ga	She'd give in.

138

Shogai ni	Never, Chrysanthemum!
Nido to wa naki	In this life a second time
Maketa Kiku	Now you've submitted!

The two foregoing probably also refer to his late courtship and marriage to Kiku, the first of his three wives.

139

Suzumera yo	Now, you Sparrows,
Shoben muyo	None of your piddling here—
Furu-fusuma	Not on our old quilts!

Bedding in Japan is probably aired no more frequently than elsewhere, but it does often appear in public with risks of the kind mentioned.

140

Muda hito ya
Hana no miyako mo
Aki no kaze

Vain Man!
To the Flowery City too
Comes an autumn wind.

141

Muda hito wo
Shikari nasaru ya

Aki no tsuki

Vain Man!
How gently does it chide you
    though
The autumn moon.

142

Uguisu ya
Ame darake naru
Asa no koe

The Nightingale—
With her morning voice
Drenched by rain.

143

Mushi naku ya
Tobu ya tenden

Ware-ware ni

The Insects chirrup—
And leap out, each one for
    itself,
Just like ourselves.

144

Inu to cho
Tanin muki de mo
Nakari keri

A Puppy, look,
And a Butterfly
No eyes for any other.

145

Rusu ni suru zo	We are going now
Koi shite asobe	Make love then to your heart's content
Io no hae	Flies at our hut!

146

Nikko no	How did it go,
Matsuri wa do da	The Festival at Nikko?
Hototogisu	O Cuckoo.

At Nikko, a long way over mountainous country from Kashiwabara, a festival accompanied by much pageantry is held in June of each year, in honour of the first Tokugawa Shogun, the great Iyeyasu, who is there buried.

147

Yabu kage ya	In the thicket's shade
Tatta hitori no	A Woman by herself
Taue uta	Sings the planting song.

148

Taue uta	The planting song . . .
Donna urami mo	How much wrangling, how much anger
Tsukinu beshi	Must it consume!

149 *On Living behind a Shop*

Suzukaze no	The cool breeze—
Magari-kunette	Comes winding and wandering
Kitarikeri	At last—it's here!

Houses in Tokyo are still set very close, and as Issa hints in his next verse this sometimes forces on one an embarrassing view of a neighbour's establishment.

150   *On the Pity of Living Upstairs*

Atsuki yo wo   The hot night through
Nirami-aitari   How we glared at each other,
Oni-gawara   Neighbour Gargoyle!

151

Ishibashi wo   With one's foot
Ashi de tazuneru   'Testing a stone bridge'
Yosamu kana   —How cold the night!

Doubtless a recollection of the famous maxim of Iyeyasu—'Never step on a stone bridge without trying it.' He was as renowned for his patience as for his success in war.

152

Mi no ue no   Heedless that the tolling bell
Kane tomo shirade   Marks our own closing day—
Yusuzumi   We take this evening's cool.

153

Nomi domo ni   Come on, Fleas,
Matsushima misete   I'll show you Matsushima—
Nigasu zo yo   Then let you go

Matsushima, literally 'Pine Islands', is a large bay near Sendai, celebrated for the hundreds of little islands of white sandstone which the sea has carved into curious shapes. Most of them have a few dark-coloured pines fantastically bent and twisted by the wind.

84

At Matsushima

Meigetsu ya
Matsu nai shima mo
Atama kazu

A radiant moon!
I can count them over too
The islets without pines.

155

Muda kusa ya
Nanji mo nobiru
Hi mo nobiru

In vain, Useless Weeds,
Do you stretch still further—
The day also stretches.

156

Mi no ue no
Tsuyu to mo shirade
Hodashikeri

Heedless of the dew
That marks our closing day
We bind ourselves to others.

157

Ominaeshi
Nan no inga ni

Karekaneru

Maiden Flower!
What destiny was it determined
You'd never fade?

158 *The Wayfarer*

Fundoshi ni
Wakizashi sashite
Fuyu no tsuki!

With a dagger
Worn in the loincloth . . .
Winter's moon!

159 *At Basho's Tomb*

Okinaki ya
Naniyara shaberu
Kado suzume

The Master's grave!
What's all that noisy chatter for
Wayside Sparrows?

Tobi hiyoro	As the Gods depart
Hiiyoro kami no	The black kites go crying, crying,
O tachige na	About their progress.

For one month of the old calendar, the Shinto deities were thought to leave their local shrines and go to Ise. The original, from the *Seventh Journal,* suggests vividly by its sound not only the crying but the wheeling of the kites as they are startled.

161

Ujigami no	When he is away!
Rusu koto sawagu	What a noise from the Crows
Karasu kana	Our village god!

162

Shiratsuyu to	Practising his flute
Shirade fue fuku	He doesn't see the white dew fall—
Tonari kana	My neighbour!

163

Baka neko ya	Fool of a Cat!
Shintai giri no	Broken beggar as he is—
Ukare koe	He shouts his joy!

164

Ozoroa no	The floating cloud that hides
Tsuki wo kumorasu	The moon in the wide sky
Ukikumo wa	
Ukiyo no susu no	Does it end as soot of this float-
Nari ya shinuran	ing world?

One of Issa's comparatively few *tanka*.

165

Muda hito ya	Vain Men!
Fuyu no tsukiyo wo	They call on it to linger
Bura bura to	This moonlit winter's night.

166

On a Rainy Night

Bonyari to	Somewhat uncertainly—
Shite mo sasuga ni	And yet it is a famous Moon indeed
Meigetsu zo	That shows tonight.

167

Nanjira mo	O sleeping birds—
Fuku wo matsu ka yo	Do you also, on the water,
Ukine tori	Look for fortune?

There is perhaps an allusion here to the varying lot of women of the town since '*ukine*' can be a euphemism for sleeping with various partners.

Uguisu mo   What with the Nightingale—
Soete gomon no   I had better make the tip
Chadai kana   Five Farthings!

169

Tsuribito no   It must disturb
Jama wo ori ori   The Angler sometimes—
Sakura kana   That Cherry Tree in flower!

170   *At Shibuya*

Shin Fuji no   Bowing with respect
Shukugi ni soyogu To Fuji revealed anew—
Ka yari kana   The smoke from our smudge!

From the Tokyo district of Shibuya, Mount Fuji still appears un-
expectedly at the end of an alley, from an upper room, or over the
great shrine dedicated to the Emperor Meiji.

171   *Tanka*

Tanoshimi mo   In Joys, O Neighbour,
Urei mo hana ni   And in our Sorrowing,
Mikazuki no   Would that we kept consonance
Sori no aitaru   As with the Flowers
Tonari wo mogana Does the Crescent Moon!

172 *In Midsummer, Returning from a journey*

Waga yado to   'Our home—'
Iu bakari de mo   Just saying that alone—
Suzushisa yo   What coolness!

173

O matsuri no   Now is the Festival—
Akai detachi   And there brave in scarlet
Tombo kana   Starts the Dragon Fly!

174 *At the Flower Show*

Makete kara   Having been beaten,
Daimyo no kiku to   I learned that the Chrysanthe-
                     mum
Shirare keri   Was His Lordship's!

175

Inu no ko mo   The Puppy too
Oote iku nari   They pelt with snowballs
Yuki tsubute   Till he scampers off!

176

Daimyo wa   His Lordship passes
Nurete toru wo   Drenched to the skin—
Kotatsu kana   And we're snug at the stove!

Furuyuki no   Even as the snow fell
Naka mo harukaze   Through it there came whisper-
                         ing
Fukinikeri   A breath of the Spring!

178

Uguisu ya   The Nightingale!
Gozen e dete mo   In His Highness's presence
                         chamber
Onaji koe   It is the same song!

179

Daimyo wo   Staring at them—
Nagamenagara no   Their Lordships as they pass
Kotatsu kana   We hug the brazier!

This doubtless alludes to the theatre where the pageantry and pre-
tension of 'high life' was as popular with the groundlings as it has
been in other countries. Issa's point is, of course, that outside the
theatre, commoners were required to sit at the side of the road in
respectful attitudes if they met a daimyo on progress until he and his
retinue had passed.

180

Gomen nari   Once in the box
Shogi no koma mo   Every one of them is privileged
Hako no naka   —The chess pieces!

The sense could also be that the chessmen are 'excused' both the duties and privileges of their ranks when laid aside. Tradition has it that Issa recited this pithy verse at one of his famous interviews with Kaga-no-Kami, the most wealthy nobleman of Japan. A more doubtful sequel, considering his evident powers of perception and literary taste, is that Kaga-no-Kami asked what the lines meant, whereupon Issa expatiated on the importance of men and women, gentles and common, before the Great Leveller.

181

Ningen ga nakuba	If there were no men
Magaraji	You wouldn't have got that twist—
Kiku no hana	Chrysanthemum!

182

In Bed

Negaeri wo	Look out!
Suru zo soko noke	I'm going to turn now—
Kirigirisu	Move over, Cricket!

183

Benten no	Before Lady Benten
Mae ni narande	They assemble and intone—
Naku kawazu	The croaking frogs.

A small wooded island on Lake Nojiri is popularly called after Benten, the Goddess of Love and Eloquence.

184

Kuraki yori	Out of the dark
Kuraki ni hairu ya	Into the darkness they go—
Neko no koi	The loves of a Cat!

185

Soko ni iyo
Heta demo
Ore ga uguisu zo

Just stay there—
You're no great singer
But you're my nightingale!

186

Tsuki chirari
Uguisu chirari
Yo wa akenu

A glimpse of the Moon—
A note from the Nightingale—
And the night's over!

187

Tabibito no
Warukuchi su nari
Hatsu shigure

What sarcasm
It offers to the Traveller—
The first bleak drizzle!

188

Kaga dono no
O saki wo tsui to
Kigisu kana

Just before the presence
Of my Lord of Kaga,
Struts a Green Pheasant!

189

Baka nagai hi ya to
Kuchi aku
Karasu kana

What a long day!
Beaks all a-gaping
So the Crows say.

190   *March 1818 . . . The Falls of Yorodaki*

Oboroyo ya
Sake no nagare shi

Taki no tsuki

The night is dim
But over the falls that ran with
    wine
Stands the moon.

Diary entry reads—'Finished off the wine last night broached on 7th July.'

One of the paragons of filial piety was a young woodcutter who denied himself necessities to provide his aged father with the strong drink that was his ruling passion. As a reward, Heaven revealed to him a cascade running with wine of peculiar excellence.

191

Ume saku ya	The plum tree blossoms
Jigoku no kama mo	And today the cauldrons of hell
Kyujitsu to	Are idle!

192

Yamabuki ya	Kerria flowers!
Shigatsu no haru mo	And that's an end already
Nakunaru ni	To April's Spring!

193

Yamayaki ya	Burning off the grass!
Butsutai to mie	One moment it seems a blessing
Oni to mie	The next, a curse!

194

Iye karu ya	We'll lend you a home,
Suzume mo kodomo	Sparrow!
Sodatsu made	Till your children are reared.

195

Hachi naite	A Bee—
Hito no shizumaru	Buzzing about the Temple Hall
Mido kana	Where folk go for peace!

196

Momo no hi ya	Peach Festival—
Fukakusa yaki no	And there, in Fukakusa, glows
Kaguya-hime	Kaguyahime!

The third day of the third month is celebrated as the Festival of Peach Blossom and is set apart for young girls, who then exhibit treasured dolls. Kaguya-hime was a fairy child, found in a shining bamboo tree by a wood-cutter and she grew up to be a maiden of rare beauty. Her wooing, the tasks set the numerous suitors who sought her hand, and her eventual return unwed, to the Courts of the Moon form the subject of the earliest Japanese romance now extant, *The Woodcutter's Tale*. *Fukakusa*, pronounced almost *Fukak'sa* and meaning literally 'deep grass' is also a place-name and was used by a famous seventeenth-century doll-maker, Kamo Kouemon, to mark the figures he made from unglazed Fushimi-ware.

197

Suppon mo	The turtle, even,
Toki ya tsukuran	May mark the time by your changes
Haru no tsuki	O Moon of Spring!

'Moon and turtle' form a proverbial contrast.

198

Tanomoshi ya	Something to depend on—
Tana no kaiko mo	That the Silkworms on their shelf
Kui zakari	Will also like their meal.

199

Shoben no	The piddle patters down
Tara tara shita ya	And underneath—look at it!
Kaki tsubata	The wild iris!

200

Yakamashi ya	What a noise you make!
Oikake oikake	Chivvying hither, chivvying thither
Hototogisu	O Cuckoo, Bird of Time!

In Heian times the cuckoo was sometimes associated with 'the hill of death'.

201

Mihotoke ya	Holy Lord Buddha!
Kojiki machi ni mo	In the Beggars' Quarter also
Go tanjo	He is born anew!

This and the following verse refer to the Festival of Flowers, on the eighth day of the fourth month, when the birthday is celebrated of Gautama, the founder of Buddhism. Among other ceremonies, tea is poured over small images of the young prince.

202

Kodomora mo　　　　　Children too,
Atama ni abiru　　　　They anoint His Head
Amacha kana　　　　　With the sweet tea of Heaven!

203

Iku na iku na　　　　　Don't go, don't go!
Ora ga nakama zo　　　I am of your company—
Kankodori　　　　　　Country cuckoo!

204

Yoi yo to ya　　　　　A good world it is, indeed!
Mushi ga suzu furi　　Where the Beetle rings his little
　　　　　　　　　　　　bell
Tobi ga mau　　　　　And the Kite pirouettes!

The suzumushi (bell-insect) is actually a kind of cricket.

205

Onozukara　　　　　　O Peony!
Atama no sagaru　　　Of itself the head is bowed
Botan kana　　　　　　Before you.

206

Mushi naku ya　　　　Insects may sing—
Ari wa damatte　　　　But the Emmet in silence
Shiribeta e　　　　　　Shows us his arse!

207

Yamazato wa　　　　　Here at the mountain village,
Shiru no naka made　Look how the fair moon
　　　　　　　　　　　　comes—
Meigetsu zo　　　　　Into our soup!

96

208

Higurashi no	Clear-toned Cicada!
Asa kara sawagu	He's made it ring from morn-ing
Yamaya kana	Our mountain house.

209

Buppo ga	Without Buddha's Law
Nakuba hikaraji	It would not shine at all
Kusa no tsuyu	This dew upon the grass!

210

Kono tsugi wa	Am I the next?
Waga mi no ue ka	Is this the body fated then
Naku karasu	O cawing Crow?

211

Hana no yo wo	A World of Flowers!
Mukan no kitsune	But the Fox in it of no degree
Naki ni keri	Howls to high heaven.

'No degree' alludes by contrast to one who was of very high degree as messenger and attendant of the Rice Goddess, and at the head of a vulpine hierarchy in the Inari cult. Other foxes were regarded, as in China, with superstitious fear as agents of magical possession and baneful to humankind. A *haiga* with the manuscript of this verse shows a weary-looking fox being driven by peasants from a snug shelter in a rice field.

Fukuro yo	Come on, Owl!
Tsura-guse naose	Come on, change that look of yours
Haru no ame	Now in the soft spring rain!

The wife of one of Issa's friends, evidently of no gentle countenance, thought that this admonition was intended for her, and was gravely offended.

213 *In Illness*

Utsukushi ya	What loveliness!
Shoji no ana no	Seen through a crack in the wall
Ama-no-gawa	The River of Heaven!

The *shoji* is, of course, the light framework of wood and thick paper that forms inner walls and screens in Japanese houses.

214

Yo ga yoku ba	If things were better,
Mo hitotsu tomare	We'd welcome one more of you—
Meshi no hae	Flies on the porridge!

215

Ima made wa	Unpunished yet
Bachi mo ataranu	I spread my net for slumber
Hirune kana	At noonday.

216

Suzume no ko
Soko noke soko noke
O uma ga toru

Fledgling Sparrows!
Make way, make way,
Way for the noble Horse!

IV · Mostly of Age

217

Omoumaji	Not to turn—
Mimaji to suredo	Not to think of it I'd determined—
Waga ya kana	But it is my home!

Towards the end of his life Issa planned to make a journey to the north and set out, but after some time began to wonder whether he would ever return. He sat down under a tree, looked back at Kashiwabara, and after some internal debate turned back.

218

Akikaze ya	Wind of Autumn!
Mushiritagarishi	And the scarlet flowers are there
Akai hana	That she loved to pluck!

The allusion is to Sato, his much-loved daughter.

219

Yuzen to shite	Composedly, he sits,
Yama wo miru	Contemplating the mountains—
Kawazu kana	The worthy frog!

220

Ko wo kakusu	Round that copse
Yabu no mawari ya	Where her chicks are hidden
Naku hibari	The lark flutters, chirping.

221

Aru toki wa
Hana no miyako ni mo

Aki ni keri

A time there was,
When even the flowery capital
   itself
Wearied this person.

222

Ro no hata ya
Yobe no warai ga
Itomagoi

Around the hearth—
The smile that bids us welcome
Is also a farewell!

223

Ware to yama
Kawarugawaru ni
Hototogisu

Myself and the Mountain—
She sings to us by turns
Does Cuckoo.

224

Yuki ni hi ya
Furusatobito mo
Buashirai

A day of snow—
And the folk of my village,
How cold are their shoulders!

Not quite, literally, but *buashirai* is slang for cold treatment. Written after a short and exasperating visit to Kashiwabara in 1806.

225

Kokoro kara
Shinano no yuki ni
Furarekeri

Chilled to the heart
By the snows of Shinano,
See me rejected!

Written on a similar occasion.

226

Namu Amida	Praise to the Buddha!
Ore ga homachi no	Here's me by blown Lettuce too—
Na mo saita	Popped up sprouting!

227 *At Soto-ga-hama*

Kyo kara wa	From today
Nihon no kari zo	You're Japan's geese, wild ones,
Raku ni neyo	Rest then in peace!

Soto-ga-hama is on the coast of what in Issa's time was the province of Mutsu and is now Aomori at the extreme west of the northern part of the main island. It is there that the wild geese migrating from Asia reach Japan and Issa is supposed to have composed this famous *haiku* while watching an approaching flock, high in the sky.

228

Uodomo ya	Fish in the butt—
Oke tomo shirade	Heedless that a butt it is
Kado suzumi	They take their evening cool.

229 *Spring*

Toshi yori mo	Getting old
Kirai tamawanu	And still they don't dislike me—
Sakura kana	Flowers of the Cherry.

New Year 1795—at Sennenji

    Ganjitsu ya   New Year's Day!
    Sara ni ryoshuku to   Not at all I'd think myself
    Omoezu   At a Travellers' Inn.

New Year 1804—at Edo

    Kakenabe mo   Old Crack-Pot!
    Asahi sasunari   The morning sun is shining
                          through
    Kore mo haru   And this once more is Spring.

Spring or 'Haru' in the *haiku* and other connections began for the
Japanese with the New Year. Thus Issa's book *Ora-ga-Haru* (literally
'My Spring') traces very roughly the cycle of a year. It begins with
a short tale of the Abbot of a certain temple, who on the last night
of the year wrote out an invitation to Paradise, addressed it to himself,
and had it delivered in public by an acolyte on New Year's morning
when it was heard by the assembled monks with much rejoicing and,
no doubt, some astonishment. Whether this was intended to encour-
age the faithful, or to demonstrate the illusion of even praiseworthy
desire does not appear, but Issa follows it with the *haiku* I have set
out hereunder which marks his wariness of the future after all the
calamity that had befallen him.

    Medetasa mo   New Year for me
    Chukurai nari   And now my Felicity
    Ora ga haru   Keeps to the mean.

233

Tomokaku mo	After all, after all,
Anata makase no	I commend myself and mine to You,
Toshi no kure	Now at the Year's end.

This *haiku*, which I have also quoted in the introduction, is the last in *Ora-ga-Haru*. It has a long prefatory note in which Issa expounds his views on religion, strongly favouring 'justification by faith'. The note ends: 'The Buddha, whether he be besought or not, will graciously perform our salvation. Here then is the truth which can alone give tranquillity to the heart.—Amen and Amen'.

234   *New Year 1805—at Edo*

Mata kotoshi	This year again
Shaba fusage zo yo	Still weigh upon the grim old earth
Kusa no iye	Hut built of straw!

235   *New Year 1806—at Edo*

Hatsu haru ya	First of the Year
Keburi tatsuru mo	Up piles the smoke again
Seken-muki	For the world fitting!

236   *New Year 1808—at Edo, lodging with Seibi*

Ume saku ya	The plum in bloom—
Aware kotoshi mo	A pity that this year again
Morai-mochi	We beg our New Year cake.

237   *New Year 1811—at Edo*

Waga haru mo	My Spring it is—
Jojokichi yo	Luck's at its tip-top now
Ume no hana	The plum has flowered!

238   *New Year 1812—at Edo—the year before his final return to Kashiwabara*

Onore yare	Well, here I am,
Ima ya goju no	Now that I've seen for fifty full years— .
Hana no haru	Spring and its Flowers!

239   *New Year 1813*

Yosonami no	As others keep them
Shogatsu mo senu	How can I keep the New Year rites—
Shidaraka na	Sloven that I am!

240   *New Year 1814—at Kashiwabara*

Assari to	The Year came
Haru wa ki ni keri	In all its simplicity
Asagizora	And azure sky.

Issa left Edo on 17th December and arrived at Kashiwabara, where Kiku greeted him, on 25th December.

241 *New Year 1817—at Sairinji in Shimosa*
ill with Scabies

Konna mi mo	Even a body such as this
Hirou kami arite	There is a god with grace to save
Hana no haru	The flowering spring!

242   *New Year 1818 in Shimosa*

Hatsuzora wo	Greet the new sky
Hayashi koso sure	With consonance of harmonies—
Suzume made	Right to the Sparrows!

243 *New Year 1821 after an Illness which had been*
expected to prove fatal

Kotoshi kara	This year and on
Marumoke zo yo	Is all pure gaining for me now—,
Shaba asobi	The world and its pleasures!

244

Kimi nakute	Without you, dear,
Makoto ni tadai no	Too many and too wide in truth—
Kodachi kana	The groves where we walked.

245

Tonari kara	From neighbours
Kinodokugaru ya	Come messages of sympathy—
Osozakura	Late-flowering Cherry!

The 'neighbours' were his stepmother, Satsu, who died in 1828, and his stepbrother of painful memory, Senroku, who died three years later. This verse was written during his last illness.

246

Mata muda ni	Uselessly again
Kuchi aku tori no	Its beak is opening
Mamako kana	The orphaned bird
(Tsubame mo Issa)	(The swallow—and Issa too)

Accompanied by a *haiga* of a swallow in flight.

247

Ume no ki ni	Little wren
Daigan aru ka	Have you some great desire to ask
Misosazai	Of the plum tree?

248

Mizudori ya	Water-fowl!
Hito wa sorezore	Men are so full of haste
Isogashiki	Each on his occasion!

249

Kane no koe	A note from the bell—
Mizutori no koe	A cry from the water-fowl—
Yo wa kuraki	And the night darkens!

250

Naka naka ni	No lightsome thing it is
Hito to umarete	To have been born a man
Aki no kure	Now autumn closes!

ORIGINAL TEXT OF POEMS

1. おらが世やそこらの草も餅になる

2. 長いぞよ夜が長いぞよなむあみだ

3. 陽炎や手に下駄はいて善光寺

4. 春風や牛に引れて善光寺

5. 名月や西に向へばぜん光寺

6. 重箱の銭四五文や夕時雨

7. 湯けぶりも月夜の春と成りにけり

8. なでしこや地蔵菩薩の迹先に

9. 蚤どもが夜永だらうぞ淋しかろ

10. 秋風やあれも昔の美少年

11.　我仏けふもいづくの草枕

12.　名月やけふはあなたも御急ぎ

13.　古犬や蚯蚓の唄にかんじ顔

14.　虫なくなそこは諸人の這入口

15.　山吹や草にかくれて又そよぐ

16.　名月は汐に流るゝ小舟かな

17.　夕暮や池なき方もさくらちる

18.　わが春は竹一本に柳哉

19.　雲の峯見越し見越して安蘇煙

20.　見かぎりし古郷の桜咲にけり

21.　野大根も花咲にけり鳴雲雀

22.　雷に鳴あはせたる雉哉

23. 女から先へかすむぞ汐干がた

24. 笠の蠅も〔う〕けふから〔は〕江戸者ぞ

25. やれ打つな蠅が手を摺り足をする

26. 雀子も梅に口明く念仏哉

27. ふる雨に一人残りし花の陰

28. 古郷の見へなくなりて鳴雲雀

29. 菫咲門や夜さえなつかしき

30. 我前に誰々住し菫ぞも

31. 雁なくや平家時分の浜の家

32. 我星は上総の空をうろつくか

33. 秋の風劔の山を来る風か

34. 秋の風我は参るはどの地獄

35. 秋の風乞食は我を見くらぶる

36. 朝寒や松は去年の松なれど

37. きりぎりす隣に居ても聞へけり

38. 白菊に拙き手水かかる也

39. 我植し松も老けり秋の暮

40. ゆり咲や大骨折て雲雀鳴

41. 何事もたのみなければなむあみだ

42. 用なしは我と葎ぞ時鳥

43. 我汝を待こと久し時鳥

44. 人は年とるべきものぞ鴫の立

45. 行先も只秋風ぞ小順礼

46. かまくらや昔どなたの千代椿

III

47. 傘さして箱根越也春の雨

48. 大井川見へてそ(れ)から雲雀哉

49. 浜松や蟬によるべの浪の声

50. 亀どのゝいくつのとしぞ不二の山

51. 義仲寺へいそぎ候はつしぐれ

52. おの〔づ〕から頭が下る神ぢ山

53. 掃溜へ鶴の下りけり和歌の浦

54. 地獄へは斯う参れとや閑古鳥

55. 大仏の鼻から出たる乙鳥哉

56. 花さくや京の美人の頰かぶり

57. 涼しさや弥陀成仏の此かたは

58. 舟が着て候とはぐふとん哉

59. 名月や蟹も平を名乗り出^{でる}

60. 涼風や力一ぱいきりぎりす

61. 夏山や一人きげんの女郎花

62. 涼しさや山から見える大座敷

63. 涼風はあなた任せぞ墓の松

64. 赤蜻蛉かれも夕が好じやゝら

65. 露の世の露の中にてけんくわ哉

66. 露ちるや後生大事に鳴く雀

67. 古郷やちさいがおれが夏木立

68. 正月やよ所に咲ても梅の花

69. 大雨や月見の舟も見へてふる

70. 目出度さは上総の蚊にも喰れけり

71. 彦星のにこにこ見ゆる木間哉

72. しやんしやんと虫もはたおりて星迎

73. 鳴な虫別るゝ恋はほしにさへ

74. 露の玉一ツ一ツに古郷あり

75. わが犬が蜻蛉返りの花の哉

76. 名月や仏のやうに膝をくみ

77. 蝉は霜夜の声を自慢哉

78. 雪とけて村一ぱいの子ども哉

79. 雀の子地蔵の袖にかくれけり

80. 鳥等も恋をせよとてやく野哉

81. 君が代は紺ののれんも桜哉

82. 一本の草も涼風やどりけり

83. 寝た犬にふはとかぶさる一葉哉

84. 露ちるや地獄の種をけふもまく

85. 世につれて花火の玉も大きいぞ

86. けふの日や信濃育も菊の花

87. もたいなや昼寝して聞田うへ唄

88. 螢見や転びながらもあれ螢

89. 夕顔や馬の尻へも一ツ咲

90. 人の世に田に作るゝ蓮の花

91. 世の中や蝶のくらしもいそがしき

92. 桜見て歩く間も小言哉

93. 山吹をさし出し顔の垣ね哉

94. いざ名乗れ松の御前ぞ時鳥

95. 涼風も仏任せの我身かな

96. 我庵は草も夏瘦したりけり

97. 是はさて寝耳に水の時鳥

98. 寝て起て大欠して猫の恋

99. さくらさくらと唄れし老木哉

100. 名月や高観音の御ひざ元

101. 赤い月是は誰のじや子ども達

102. 山人は鍬を枕や鳴雲雀

103. 世〔の〕中は地獄の上の花見哉

104. それでこそ御時鳥松の月

105. 我死なば墓守となれきりぎりす

106. 古犬が先に立也はか参り

107. 下谷一番の顔してころもがへ

108. 短夜ややよやといふこそ人も花

109. 鶯よ江戸の氷室は何が咲

110. 初蟬といへば小便したりけり

111. 三日月とそりがあふやら時鳥

112. 君が代は女もす也冬籠り

113. 鳴な雁どつこも同じうき世ぞや

114. 七転び八起の花よ女郎花

115. 鶯や泥足ぬぐふ梅の花

116. 犬の子の加へて寝たる柳哉

117. 夜神楽や焚火の中へちる紅葉

118. 苦の娑婆や桜が咲ば咲いたとて

119.　卯の花や神と乞食の中に咲

120.　かくれ家や歯のない口で福は内

121.　しなのちや雪が消れば蚊がさはぐ

122.　春雨や喰はれ残りの鴨が鳴

123.　大猫よはやく行け行け妻が鳴

124.　我宿は鼠と仲のよい螢

125.　正月や梅のかはりの大吹雪

126.　だまれ蟬今髭どのがござるぞよ

127.　前の世のおれがいとこか閑古鳥

128.　蚤の迹それもわかきはうつくしき

129.　下駄からりからり夜永のやつら哉

130.　うそ寒や親といふ字を知てから

131.　菊さくや馬糞山も一けしき

132.　さる人が真丸に寝るふとん哉

133.　只頼め頼めと露のこぼれけり

134.　よい世じやと露がざんぶりざんぶり哉

135.　有明や梅にも一ツ鉢たゝき

136.　妻乞や秘若い鹿でなし

137.　大菊や負るそぶりはなかりしが

138.　生涯に二度とはなき負たきく

139.　雀らよ小便無用古衾

140.　むだ人や花の都も秋の風

141.　むだ人を叱なさるや秋の月

142.　鶯や雨だらけなる朝の声

143. 虫鳴くやとぶやてんでん我々に

144. 犬と蝶他人むきでもなかりけり

145. 留守にするぞ恋して遊べ庵の蠅

146. 日光の祭りはどうだ時鳥

147. 藪陰やたつた一人の田植唄

148. 田植歌どんな恨も尽ぬべし

149. 涼風の曲りくねつて来たりけり

150. 暑き夜〔を〕にらみ合たり鬼瓦

151. 石橋を足で尋る夜寒哉

152. 身の上の鐘ともしらで夕涼

153. 蚤どもに松島見せて逃すぞよ

154. 名月や松ない島も天窓数

155. むだ草や汝も伸る日も伸る

156. 身の上の露ともしらでほだしけり

157. 女郎花何の因果に枯かねる

158. ふんどしに脇ざしさして冬の月

159. 翁忌や何やらしやべる門雀

160. 鳶ひよろひゝよろ神の御立げな

161. 氏神の留守事さはぐ烏哉

162. 白露としらで笛吹隣哉

163. ばか猫や身体ぎりのうかれ声

164. 大空の月をくもらすうき雲は
うき世の煤のなりやしぬらん

165. むだ人や冬の月夜をぶらぶらと

166. ぼんやりとしてもさすがに名月ぞ

167. 汝等も福を待かよ浮寝鳥

168. 鶯も添て五文の茶代哉

169. 釣人の邪魔を折々桜哉

170. 新富士の祝義にそよぐ蚊やり哉

171. 楽みもうれひも花に三ケ月の
    そりの合たる隣をも哉

172. 我宿といふばかりでも涼しさよ

173. 御祭の赤い出立（でたち）蜻蛉哉

174. 負てから大名の菊としられけり

175. 犬の子も追ふて行也雪礫

176. 大名は濡れ〔て〕通るを巨燵哉

177. 降雪の中も春風吹にけり

178. 鶯や御前へ出ても同じ声

179. 大名をながめながらの巨燵哉

180. 御免なり将棋の駒も箱の中

181. 人間がなくば曲らじ菊の花

182. 寝返りをするぞそこのけ蟋

183. 弁天の前に並んでなく蛙

184. 闇より闇に入るや猫の恋

185. そこに居よ下手でもおれが鶯〔ぞ〕

186. 月ちらり鶯ちらり夜は明ぬ

187. 旅人の悪口す也初時雨

188. 加賀どのゝ御先をついと雉哉

189. ばか長い日やと口明く烏哉

190. 朧夜や酒の流し滝の月

191. 梅咲くや地獄の釜も休日と

192. 山吹や四月の春もなくなるに

193. 山焼や仏体と見へ鬼と見へ

194. 家かるや雀も子ども育〔つ〕迄

195. 蜂鳴て人のしづまる御堂哉

196. 桃の日や深草焼のかぐや姫

197. スッポンも時や作らん春の月

198. たのもしや棚の蚕も喰盛

199. 小便のたらたら下や杜若

200. やかましや追かけ追かけ時鳥

201. 御仏や乞食丁にも御誕生

202. 子どもらも天窓に浴る甘茶哉

203. 行な行なおらが仲間ぞ閑古鳥

204. よい世とや虫が鈴ふり鳶がまふ

205. おのづから頭の下るぼたん哉

206. 虫鳴や蟻はだまって尻べたへ

207. 山里は汁の中迄名月ぞ

208. 日ぐらしの朝からさはぐ山家哉

209. 仏法がなく〔ば〕光らじ草の露

210. 此次は我身の上かなく烏

211. 花の世を無官の狐鳴にけり

212. 梟よ面癖直せ春の雨

213. うつくしやせうじの穴の天〔の〕川

214. 世がよくばも一ツ留れ飯の蠅

215. 今迄は罰もあたらぬ昼寝哉

216. 雀の子そこのけそこのけ御馬が通る

217. 思ふまじ見まじとすれど我家哉

218. 秋風やむしりたがりし赤い花

219. ゆうぜんとして山を見る蛙哉

220. 子をかくす藪の廻りや鳴雲雀

221. 或時は花の都にも倦にけり

222. 炉のはたやよべの笑ひがいとまごひ

223. 我と山かはるがはるに時鳥

224. 雪の日や古郷人もぶあしらひ

225. 心からしなのゝ雪に降られけり

226. なむあみだおれがほまちの菜も咲た

227. けふからは日本の雁ぞ楽に寝よ

228. 魚どもや桶ともしらで門涼み

229. としよりも嫌ひ給はぬ桜哉

230. 元日やさらに旅宿とおもほへず

231. 欠鍋も旭さす也是も春

232. 目出度さもちう位也おらが春

233. ともかくもあなた任せのとしの暮

234. 又ことし娑婆塞ぞよ草の家

235. はつ春やけぶり立るも世間むき

236. 梅咲くやあはれことしももらひ餅

237. 我春も上々吉よ梅の花

238. おのれやれ今や五十の花の春

239. よ所並の正月もせぬしだら哉

240. あつさりと春は来にけり浅黄空

241. こんな身も拾ふ神ありて花〔の〕春

242. 初空をはやしこそすれ雀迄

243. ことしから丸儲ぞよ娑婆遊び

244. 君なくて誠に多太の木立哉

245. 隣から気〔の〕毒がるや遅ざくら

246. 又むだに口明く鳥のまゝ子哉

247. 梅の木に大願あるかみそさゝい

248. 水鳥や人はそれぞれいそがしき

249. 鐘の声水鳥の声夜はくらき

250. なかなかに人と生れて秋の暮

SELECTED BIBLIOGRAPHY

Works

Bunka Kucho. Pub. Kokin Shoin, Tokyo, 1928. (Vol. 6 in series of Issa's works edited by Shinano Educational Association.)

Issa Shichiban Nikki (*The Seventh Journal*), ed. Ogiwara. Pub. Kaizosha, Tokyo, 1931.

Ora-ga-Haru, ed. Ogiwara. Pub. Iwanami Shoten, Tokyo, 1927.

Issa Zenshu (*Collected Verse*), ed. Ohashi. Pub. Shunshusha, Tokyo, 1929.

Issa Ibokukan (Haiga and Manuscripts), ed. and printed privately for the Issa Society, Nagano, 1912.

Commentary: Japanese

Nihon Bungaku Koza (pub. 1934), Vol. 8, 'Issa Kenkyu Yosetsu'.

Nihon Bungaku: Sakuhin oyobi Sakka, Vol. 6, 'Issa Yosetsu'.

Issa Matsuri, ed. Wakatsuki & published under the auspices of the Haikaiji Issa Hozonkai.

Issa wo Tazunete. Pub. 1955 by the Nagano Educational Association.

(Essays in the publications listed under 'Works').

Commentary: English

Asiatic Society of Japan: Transactions . . . Reprints, Vol. I, 1925; 'Basho and the Japanese Epigram', by B. H. Chamberlain. *Transactions: Second Series*, Vol. IX, 1932; 'Issa's Life and Poetry', by Max Bickerton.

The Bamboo Broom, by Harold Gould Henderson. Published 1934, by Houghton Mifflin Co., New York.

Haiku Poems: Ancient and Modern, by Asataro Miyamori. Published by Maruzen, Tokyo, 1940.

Haiku, by R. H. Blyth. Vol. 1, pub. Kamakura Bunko, 1949; Vol. 2, pub. Hokuseido, 1950; Vol. 3, pub. Hokuseido, 1952; Vol. 4, pub. Hokuseido, 1952.

Japanese Literature, by Donald Keene (Wisdom of the East Series). Pub. John Murray, 1954.

1. 320±
   a. 5 weeks from March 21

INDEX

To subjects of the haiku *translated. Figures refer to poems, not pages; those prefixed by the letter 'P' refer to verses included in the Introduction*

136